The Path of Prayer

JOHN H. MORRIS

THE CHRISTADELPHIAN
404 SHAFTMOOR LANE
BIRMINGHAM B28 8SZ, UK

2004

First published 2004

ISBN 0 85189 163 2

Printed in England by
THE CROMWELL PRESS
TROWBRIDGE
WILTSHIRE
ENGLAND
BA14 0XB

THE PATH OF PRAYER

PREFACE

GOD has graciously implanted within man the instinct of prayer which enables us to communicate with our Maker. In the present age it may seem that prayer is a one-sided conversation, yet we can be confident that God hears us; He accepts our worship; He listens to our petitions and—more often than we usually care to acknowledge—He answers us. Not all have the desire to pray to God but those who do, and who commit themselves to God's service, are able to come through the Lord Jesus Christ into the presence of a Heavenly Father who hears and responds according to His infinite wisdom and compassionate love.

This work is based on articles which appeared in *The Christadelphian* from February 2002 to November 2003, though with some rearrangement and expansion. A book on prayer can never be exhaustive: more examples could have been cited of men and women of prayer in the Bible; many more verses of Scripture could have been quoted to illustrate our subject.

Some may come to this book with a lifetime's experience of prayer; others may be just beginning to understand the wonder of the privilege we have to speak with God. It is hoped that there will be something here for all readers and that with God's blessing we shall all gain greater insight into this vital aspect of our discipleship.

JOHN MORRIS

BIBLE VERSIONS: Most Scripture passages are quoted in the Authorised (King James) Version. Where other versions are used they are indicated by abbreviations, e.g. RV (Revised Version); ESV (English Standard Version).

HYMNS: Verses from several hymns are quoted from the 2002 edition of the *Christadelphian Hymn Book*.

FOREWORD

THE Lord's disciples knew they needed to learn about prayer: "Lord, teach us to pray", they asked, "as John also taught his disciples". They made their request out of a feeling of inadequacy, and because they witnessed their Master constantly directing his thoughts towards his Father in heaven. Together with reading daily from God's word, and meeting as often as possible with fellow disciples, prayer forms part of the believer's armoury as he seeks to live soberly, righteously, and godly, in this present world.

The benefits of prayer are often felt during periods of hardship, despair and difficulty, yet they are certainly not restricted to times of trouble. Prayer involves thanksgiving and rejoicing as much as it expresses distress and importunity. God has spoken to mankind through His word, and by means of prayer it is possible for men and women to respond by lifting up their hearts to Him, seeking for grace.

This short work shows how prayer was an integral part of the lives of those whose experiences have been recorded in the Scriptures for our learning. Some of the principles about prayer are discussed, and they are illustrated by Biblical examples. Equally some of the problems of prayer are addressed: How should I pray? Why is it hard for me to pray? What part does the Lord Jesus play in my prayers? How should I address the Father? When should I pray?

But the real value of this book is that it encourages us all to draw closer to God. However diffuse our thoughts, and however stumbling our language, we are assured that the Father desires His children to speak to Him in prayer. And only by praying shall we learn to pray. Perhaps that was what Jesus taught his disciples.

MICHAEL ASHTON

CONTENTS

1

FELLOWSHIP WITH GOD

Prayer is communication between man and his Maker. All down the ages, believers have come before God with their petitions, thanks and praise, and they have learned with wonder and gratitude that He hears and answers prayer.

MAN is made to communicate with God. We were created in His image and from the very beginning it was ordained that we should "feel after him and find him, though he be not far from every one of us" (Acts 17:27). The capacity for prayer is one of the attributes which distinguishes mankind from the rest of creation.

Prayer is an instinct formed within us from an early age, a natural extension of the ability and desire we have to communicate with our earthly parents. And just as we learned to speak by listening to our parents, so we shall learn to pray by listening to our Heavenly Father—and by following the examples of men and women down the ages, whose prayers are recorded for us in the Bible.

What is Prayer?

What is the definition of prayer? The English verb "to pray" means 'to ask, beg or request'. A glance at Bible lexicons tells us that the various original Hebrew and Greek words have these same meanings, but also others—for example, 'to intercede', 'to judge self', 'to bow down', 'to meditate'. Where the noun "prayer" occurs in Scripture, it too has wider meanings than just 'petition' or 'request': one Hebrew word carries the meaning of 'meditation'; another,

1

'song of praise'; and one of the words used in the New Testament suggests the idea of 'pouring out'.

We shall return in chapter 5 to some of these words and meanings. For the moment the conclusion we can draw is that prayer is very much more than merely the asking of a favour, or the stating of a request. We are in fact led to the understanding that, in its widest definition, prayer is the word that sums up praise, thanks, worship, petition, and meditation—all that man is able to offer as he seeks to approach and reverence the Almighty God. And prayer is, of course, a two-way process, for God hears and responds— He answers prayer.

Praise ... Petition ... Meditation

Let us test our definitions by examining a few verses from one of the Psalms of David, noting the range of different expressions (in italics) which convey the idea of prayer:

> "Give ear to *my words*, O LORD,
>   Consider *my meditation*.
> Hearken unto *the voice of my cry*, my King, and my
>   God:
>   For unto thee will I *pray*.
> *My voice* shalt thou hear in the morning, O LORD;
>   In the morning will I *direct my prayer* unto thee,
>   and will *look up* ...
> As for me, I will *come into thy house* in the multitude
>   of thy mercy:
> And in thy fear will I *worship toward thy holy temple*."
>   (Psalm 5:1-7)

The preoccupations of being a shepherd, soldier, fugitive or king did not prevent David from being constantly in communication with his God. On occasions of formal worship according to the Law, he would direct his prayers towards the sanctuary—there was as yet no temple, and the ark of God was in a tent. But it is not just formal worship that David has in mind in this psalm: he communes with God at many other times, asking Him to hearken to the voice of his cry; David would look up to the heavens in silent worship; he would bow his head in quiet meditation—all this is prayer. Prayer is the vehicle for all that man would bring in devotion to God.

Why pray?—and why should God hear us?

In our study of prayer, then, we are reflecting particularly on the relationship between God and man. But questions arise immediately: Why should the Holy and Eternal One deign to listen to us? What can God gain from our supplications? Why should we presume that He will respond to our cries? It is indeed a miracle that man can converse with God, a privilege we can treat too lightly. But it is clear that the Almighty Maker of heaven and earth *wants* us to seek Him, and has promised to listen and respond.

Why does God want us to pray? By praying we demonstrate our desire to be close to Him, to listen to our Father as we read His Word; as we pray, we show our submission to His will. But God also wishes us to pray so that we shall search our hearts and articulate what we are really thinking, and what we really desire.

How much do we know about prayer? It is a topic which is not given great prominence in our instruction for baptism, and often it may simply be assumed that experience of family prayers at home and communal prayers in the ecclesia will have given us all the grounding we need. It is true that prayer cannot be taught as we would teach Bible history, or even basic doctrines, yet there are principles to be learned and examples to be followed. By the day of our baptism we shall not be fully competent in prayer, but this is an aspect of our discipleship that develops and matures—and for many of us it is only in later years that the full wonder of prayer is appreciated.

The path of prayer opens out before every child of God: some step out confidently, if humbly, on that path; others seem reluctant to make a start and, even after many years, have not progressed very far—or have lost their way. It is a challenge for all of us to seek to enliven and strengthen this vital and rewarding part of our lives in Christ.

3

The ultimate and finest example of a man of prayer is, of course, the Lord Jesus Christ: from him—even more than from David—we learn that prayer is not an occasional brief petition, but a life in constant communion with the Father. That is the pinnacle of perfection to which our study must lead, but we cannot start there.

Before and after the Fall

As is true for so many divine principles, the place to start is Genesis. The words "pray" and "prayer" do not occur in the earliest chapters of the book, and yet man is quite evidently communicating with the Almighty. Having made the man and his wife, "God blessed them, and God *said unto them* ..." (1:28). Though not recorded as a conversation, there is clearly a dialogue here between man and God—man's part being perhaps no more than silent acceptance of the divine instructions. But if prayer is communication between man and his Maker, then this is prayer.

A very significant dialogue took place after the first transgression, when Adam and Eve "heard the voice of the LORD God walking in the garden in the cool of the day" (3:8). An inquisition followed, as the man and woman tried to defend their actions, and were banished—a flaming sword separating them from the paradise where they had so freely conversed with the LORD. As a consequence, by the end of chapter 3 of Genesis, the close communion which had existed between God and man ceased. In Eden, life had been perfect fellowship with God—one might say, a state of perfect prayer. That fellowship was now broken.

A Gulf between Man and God

What happened after the Fall? Though Adam and Eve were banished from the Garden, the way of access to God was not altogether barred, and men and women continued to speak with God. The difference was, of course, that sin had now been introduced and man had fallen from that state of intimate fellowship with his Creator. The history of mankind which the Bible records from this point onwards, is the account of the way by which that fellowship would ultimately be restored. In patriarchal times, the development of a system of priesthood signalled man's need for help in finding a way of approach to God.

Later, the Law of Moses provided a more elaborate framework for worship, prayer, and forgiveness of sins—a means for unworthy man to come into the divine presence. The tabernacle was the place appointed: "There I will meet with thee, and I will commune with thee from above the mercy seat" (Exodus 25:22). Yet even so, the gulf between man and God remained.

Only with the coming of the Son of God, and through his perfect sacrifice, was the means found by which we could enjoy lasting reconciliation with our God. As a result, we may now have "boldness to enter into the holiest by the blood of Jesus, by a new and living way". Reconciled to God, we can "draw near with a true heart in full assurance of faith" (Hebrews 10:19,20,22). These are words which describe our present privileged relationship with God, but there is a still higher state to which we can aspire.

"The tabernacle of God is with men"

The fulness of true prayer will one day be granted when "the tabernacle of God is with men, and he will dwell with them, and they shall be his people, and God himself shall be with them, and be their God" (Revelation 21:3). In that day, by God's grace, faltering prayer will be transformed into perfection of fellowship between God and man.

Prayer is the soul's sincere desire,
  Uttered or unexpressed;
The motion of a hidden fire
  That trembles in the breast.

Prayer is the simplest form of speech
  That infant lips can try;
Prayer the sublimest strains that reach
  The Majesty on high.

The saints in prayer appear as one
  In word, in deed, and mind,
While with the Father and the Son
  Sweet fellowship they find.

O thou by whom we come to God,
  The Life, the Truth, the Way,
The path of prayer thyself hath trod,
  Lord, teach us how to pray.

HYMN 164

2

CALLING ON THE NAME
OF THE LORD

The faithful in Israel cried to God: they called upon His Name. And the same privilege now belongs to us, as Gentile believers, for in Christ we may approach the Father, "of whom the whole family in heaven and earth is named".

PATRIARCHAL times give us an insight into the pattern of worship and prayer that developed after the Fall, in spite of the estrangement between man and God brought about by sin. It is clear from Genesis that Cain and Abel had a desire to worship and the fact that Abel, at least, brought an acceptable offering shows that Adam and Eve had taught their sons the proper way of approach to God—even if Cain chose to ignore it (Genesis 4:3-5). A reading of Genesis shows how the faithful learned to pray, worship, and give glory and thanks to God.

Two-way Communication

We tend to think of prayer as a one-sided exercise, simply because we receive no audible answer to our prayers. In those earlier times, two-way communication took place, God (or an angel) speaking in conversation with man:

> "The word of the LORD came unto Abram in a vision, saying, Fear not, Abram: I am thy shield, and thy exceeding great reward. And Abram said, Lord GOD, what wilt thou give me ... ?"   (Genesis 15:1,2)

This is not the place to explore the names and titles of God, but we note as we read the early books of the Bible, how believers addressed God in various ways. We, too, can approach God with different forms of address: one brother may commence his prayer: 'Lord God Almighty'; another may start: 'Great God our Creator' or 'Gracious Father in heaven'. By adopting different ways of addressing God we avoid the staleness that might come from a stereotyped approach, but also have opportunity to marvel at the many faceted character of our God and His attributes. Such forms of address must be used reverently, and never with the intention of claiming superior knowledge or seeking to be divisive by choosing one particular form rather than another.

Calling upon God in Prayer

In our search for information on prayer in the early chapters of Scripture, the statement that we find at the end of Genesis 4 is of particular significance: "Then began men to call upon the name of the LORD". What precisely do these words mean? The AV translation suggests the obvious meaning—that men lifted up their voices to call upon God in prayer, but we shall see that there may be more behind this statement.

The first explicit reference to prayer in Genesis comes in chapter 20, where Abraham prayed unto God for Abimelech (20:7,17). Yet from the statement in Genesis 4:26, and from the references to the altars which the patriarchs built, it is clear that prayer—as part of a comprehensive system of sacrifice and worship—was in existence much earlier than this: "Noah builded an altar unto the LORD ... and offered burnt offerings on the altar" (8:20). "Abram builded an altar unto the LORD, and called upon the name of the LORD" (12:8; 13:4; cf. 21:33).

So men continued to call on the name of the LORD. Following the pattern of his ancestors, "David built (in the threshing floor of Ornan the Jebusite) an altar ... and called upon the LORD" (1 Chronicles 21:26). Elijah, taunting the prophets of Baal, said, "Call ye on the name of your gods, and I will call on the name of the LORD: and the God that answereth by fire, let him be God" (1 Kings 18:24).

As we would expect, the psalms contain an abundance of such expressions: "In my distress I called upon the LORD, and cried unto my God" (18:6); "LORD, I have called daily upon thee, I have stretched out my hands unto thee" (88:9). Psalm 116 is particularly interesting: here, "call upon" is one of a number of synonymous expressions for prayer:

> "I love the LORD, because he hath heard
>   my *voice* and my *supplications*.
> Because he hath inclined his ear unto me,
>   Therefore will I *call upon* him as long as I live …
> Then *called I upon* the name of the LORD;
>   O LORD, I *beseech* thee, deliver my soul …
> What shall I *render* unto the LORD
>   For all his benefits toward me?
> I will take the cup of salvation,
>   And *call upon* the name of the LORD.
> I will *pay my vows* unto the LORD …
> I will *offer* to thee the sacrifice of thanksgiving,
>   And will *call upon* the name of the LORD."

(Psalm 116:1,2,4,12-14,17)

Invoking God's Name

It seems clear, then, that to "call upon" God is to pray to Him, to invoke or to proclaim His Name. Just two quotations from the prophets confirm this. From Isaiah—"In that day shall ye say, Praise the LORD, *call upon* his name, declare his doings among the people, make mention that his name is exalted" (12:4). And from Jeremiah—"Then shall ye *call upon* me, and ye shall go and pray unto me, and I will hearken unto you. And ye shall seek me, and find me, when ye shall search for me with all your heart" (29:12,13).

It is interesting, incidentally, to see a similar form of words used by Paul when he refers to the saints in Christ at Corinth and elsewhere, "with all that in every place *call upon* the name of Jesus Christ our Lord, both theirs and ours" (1 Corinthians 1:2)—a Hebrew idiom now applied in a Greek context.

But there is another, and possibly deeper meaning to be found in the verse with which we began, Genesis 4:26. Many Bibles have, against the phrase, "call upon the name of the LORD", a marginal note giving the alternative "Or, to call themselves by the name of the LORD". This alternative does not do away with the first idea of praying to God and invoking His Name, but expands upon it: it suggests that in their prayers those God-fearers were not only seeking to communicate with God, but wanting to be associated with His Name. They had their own personal names but wished to be distinguished by God's Name. It is certainly significant that, from chapter 5 onwards, we start to find names constructed with 'el', and later with 'jah'—names of God incorporated into countless Hebrew personal names.

Called by the Name of the LORD

This leads to a rewarding study, taking us into other parts of Scripture. Clearly it was God's intention that His people should bear His Name: "They shall put my name upon the children of Israel" (Numbers 6:27); "All people of the earth shall see that thou art called by the name of the LORD" (Deuteronomy 28:10). But it is particularly in Isaiah that the beautiful theme of the divine name in us is worked out. In one place, the idea is expressed in no fewer than four different ways: "One shall say, I am the LORD's; and another shall call himself by the name of Jacob; and another shall subscribe with his hand unto the LORD, and surname himself by the name of Israel" (Isaiah 44:5; see also 43:1,7; 45:4; 48:1,2; 63:19).

And, again, the idea is not just to be discovered in the Old Testament: it is there in the New Testament as well. Paul—in the context of prayer—speaks of the saints taking on the divine name: "For this cause I bow my knees unto the Father of our Lord Jesus Christ, *of whom the whole family in heaven and earth is named*" (Ephesians 3:14,15; cf. Revelation 3:12).

The exhortation for all God's servants is that we should "call upon the name of the LORD"—both in the literal sense of approaching Him in quiet recognition of His mercy and

His mighty power, and in the additional sense of being identified with God's Name and purpose.

Crying unto God

In praying to the Almighty, we acknowledge our dependence upon Him, our helplessness in His sight. Out of our great need we call upon Him, confident that He will help. That is why God's servants *"cry* unto" Him. In Egypt, "the children of Israel sighed by reason of the bondage, and they cried, and their cry came up unto God" (Exodus 2:23). "Our fathers … cried unto thee, and were delivered: they trusted in thee, and were not confounded" (Psalm 22:4,5).

Individuals, too, cried to God in their time of need: "I cried unto the LORD with my voice; with my voice unto the LORD did I make my supplication. I poured out my complaint before him" (Psalm 142:1,2).

But there were times when it seemed that God did not hear. Jeremiah laments: "When I cry and shout, he shutteth out my prayer" (Lamentations 3:8,44). And centuries before, of course, there was Job who poured out his complaint and wondered why God appeared not to answer him: "Behold, I cry out of wrong, but I am not heard: I cry aloud, but there is no judgment" (19:7). (Here, "cry out" is the more common expression; "cry aloud" expresses Job's feelings more strongly.)

"Oh that I knew where I might find him!"

Job was "perfect and upright, one that feared God, and eschewed evil" (1:1), but the calamities that came upon him revealed a man who had not matured in his relationship with God. At one stage, in his bitterness, he cries, "What is the Almighty, that we should serve him? And what profit should we have, if we pray unto him?" (21:15). On the other hand, he is keen to argue with God: "Surely I would speak to the Almighty, and I desire to reason with God" (13:3). "Oh that I knew where I might find him, that I might come even to his seat! I would order my cause before him, and fill my mouth with arguments" (23:3,4).

Because of his contentious attitude, the LORD had to rebuke him: "Shall a fault-finder contend with the Almighty? He who argues with God, let him answer it" (40:2, ESV). Job had not learned the virtue of a meek and quiet spirit. As a result of his experiences, however, he discovered a new relationship with God: in the end, Job acknowledges that he had spoken hastily and bows in contrition before his God:

> "Behold, I am of small account; what shall I answer thee? I lay mine hand upon my mouth ... I uttered that which I understood not, things too wonderful for me, which I knew not ... Wherefore I abhor myself, and repent in dust and ashes."   (Job 40:4; 42:3-6, RV)

Learning about Ourselves, and about God

By communing with God we learn more about Him and also about ourselves: this is one of the purposes of prayer. Job, through his experiences, and also through his dialogue with God, learned more about himself, and more about the Almighty. No longer was Job crying aloud in his distress and challenging God to answer him: instead he had learned to accept, if not always to understand, God's ways. In effect, he had learned not just to cry aloud, but to pray.

Moreover, the one who pleaded for a "daysman" (9:33) now himself becomes a mediator on behalf of the three friends: "My servant Job shall pray for you: for him will I accept ... And the LORD turned the captivity of Job, when he prayed for his friends" (42:8,10).

None of us would wish to endure the trials which Job suffered, yet even our "light afflictions" will help us to learn to be humble before our Maker; to stop and think before we challenge God's wisdom, and to accept His will.

3

A SWEET SMELLING SAVOUR

Acceptable sacrifices arose to God as a "sweet smelling savour". Incense, too, gave a pleasing fragrance and became symbolic of prayer. Our prayers, sincerely presented in Christ's name, arise as a sweet savour to the throne of grace.

WHEN Abraham and Isaac journeyed to Moriah, in obedience to the divine command to offer Isaac as a sacrifice, Abraham said to his young men: "Abide ye here with the ass; and I and the lad will go yonder and worship, and come again to you" (Genesis 22:5). The object of their mission was sacrifice, yet Abraham describes it as "worship".

Patriarchal Worship

Later, when Abraham sent his eldest servant to the city of Nahor to seek a wife for Isaac, and Rebekah spoke graciously to him by the well, "the man bowed down his head, and worshipped the LORD" (24:26,48); and again, when Laban and Bethuel consented to give Rebekah as a wife for Isaac, the servant once more "worshipped the LORD, bowing himself to the earth" (verse 52). For Abraham's servant, the instinctive reaction to a circumstance in which he saw the hand of God was to worship: the God of Abraham must first be acknowledged. How often we overlook the need *first* to acknowledge God's work in our lives!

The striking thing about these verses is that they contain the only explicit references to "worship" in the book of Genesis. Does that mean that in earlier times worship was not understood or practised? Did Adam and Eve not worship the LORD God? Did worship not form a part of the lives of Seth and his descendants? We explored in chapter 2 the meaning of the statement, "Then began men to call upon the name of the LORD" (Genesis 4:26) and concluded that in calling upon God they were actually engaged in acts of worship and prayer.

An Acceptable Offering

When Noah came forth from the ark, did he worship? It is inconceivable that this righteous man should forget to give thanks and praise: he and his family had, after all, been saved from death by the mercy of God, and bound in an eternal covenant. Worship is not mentioned as such, yet there is a phrase which more than suggests it: when Noah built an altar and offered burnt offerings, "the LORD smelled a sweet* savour" (8:21). By his actions, at least, and surely in words as well, Noah had expressed his gratitude to God—and God accepted his worship. Noah may even have petitioned God never again to bring such a catastrophe upon the earth. When the LORD promised, "I will not again curse the ground ... neither will I again smite any more every thing living", this may well have been the answer to a specific prayer on Noah's part.

So there is, in Genesis, clear evidence that the patriarchs prayed and worshipped. Indeed, in the next chapter, which records the blessings and cursings on Shem, Ham and Japheth, Noah says, "*Blessed be* the LORD, the God of Shem" (9:26, RV): here is an expression of worship, which came naturally to Noah. The faithful patriarchs lived in close communication with God, and even if the Genesis record does not always say so explicitly, they were constant in their worship. They were men of prayer.

---

*The Hebrew word translated "sweet" is *nichoach*, which is very close to *noach* (or Noah), meaning 'rest'. There is in Genesis 8 a delightful interplay of meaning between the name "Noah" (*rest*), the phrase "the ark *rested*" (8:4), and "a *sweet* savour" (or "savour of *rest*"; 8:21, AV margin).

Sacrifice and Incense

Noah's sacrifices foreshadowed the countless offerings under the Law of Moses, whose fragrance would rise to God as a sweet smelling savour. The morning and evening sacrifices, for example, were to be "for a sweet savour, an offering made by fire unto the LORD" (Exodus 29:41; Numbers 28:8). The savour would, of course, arise from the burning of the sacrificial animal, enhanced by the accompanying flour, oil and wine—a fragrance pleasing to Almighty God. The aroma which rose heavenwards was a token of the Israelite's worship; the sacrifice was, in a sense, a prayer.

Yet there was something in the Law of Moses which came more particularly to represent prayer: the offering of incense. Morning and evening (Exodus 30:7,8), "sweet* incense" had to be burned, which itself of course would lend further fragrance to the daily offerings. On the Day of Atonement, moreover, the high priest was to take a censer full of burning coals, "and his hands full of sweet* incense beaten small ... and he shall put the incense upon the fire before the LORD, that the cloud of the incense may cover the mercy seat" (Leviticus 16:12,13).

What could be a more fitting symbol of prayer? Through the high priest, the supplications and worship of the people, and their desire for forgiveness, were being brought to God in the place of which He had promised, "There will I meet with thee, and I will commune with thee from above the mercy seat" (Exodus 25:22). The Israelites might just see the vapours of burning incense mingling in the pillar of cloud above the tabernacle—and the perceptive ones would understand the lesson.

David certainly understood the spiritual meaning of incense. He was conscious of the commandment to offer sacrifices and burn incense morning and evening, and at other times, but for him that was not all:

*These occurrences of "sweet" are translations of another Hebrew word, *sammim*.

15

"Let my *prayer* be set forth before thee as *incense*; and the lifting up of my hands as the evening sacrifice."

(Psalm 141:2)

Like every truly God-fearing Israelite, he did not leave it just to the priests to perform this daily ritual: morning and evening, David would personally come before God in prayer. The writer to the Hebrews surely has this psalm in mind when he exhorts:

"Through him then let us offer up a sacrifice of praise to God continually, that is, the fruit of lips which make confession to his name." (13:15, RV)

The Book of Revelation, too, confirms the connection between incense and prayer:

"The four living creatures and the four and twenty elders fell down before the Lamb, having each one a harp, and golden bowls full of *incense* (odours, AV), which are the *prayers* of the saints." (5:8, RV; cf. 8:3,4)

A Life Well Pleasing to God

But there are two other New Testament passages, both from the pen of Paul, which add a further dimension to the idea of a sweet smelling savour. To the Philippians, the apostle writes:

"I am full, having received of Epaphroditus the things which were sent from you, *an odour of a sweet smell*, a sacrifice acceptable, well pleasing to God." (4:18)

Paul perceived what the Law was really trying to teach: that the Israelite was not just to go through the ritual of bringing sacrifices, and offering incense, but to devote all that he had—in fact, himself—to God. And the same must apply to those not under the Law. The One who did this fully and to perfection was the Lord Jesus Christ, who "loved us, and hath given himself for us, an offering and a sacrifice to God *for a sweetsmelling savour*" (Ephesians 5:2). His whole life was a prayer—as ours should be.

16

4

ANGELS, PRIESTS AND PROPHETS

In Old Testament times, God revealed Himself through angels, priests and prophets: these were God's intermediaries when He spoke to His people. For us, the Lord Jesus Christ has opened a "new and living way" of access to God.

PRAYER is communication between man and God. When David says, for example, "Hear my cry, O God; attend unto my prayer" (Psalm 61:1), he is taking advantage of man's privileged access to the Almighty. David speaks direct to God; and, like countless faithful men and women before him and since, he trusted that his prayer would be heard.

Old Testament Prophets

But, in fact, we are over-simplifying the position of David. It is true that the psalms portray an intimate relationship with God, but the historical record also shows David using the proper priestly arrangements of the time, and also communicating with God through the prophets of his day. After his sin with Bathsheba and the death of Uriah, God sent the prophet Nathan to David with a parable and with the accusation, "Thou art the man". "David said unto Nathan, I have sinned against the LORD. And Nathan said unto David, The LORD also hath put away thy sin" (2 Samuel 12:1-13). The dialogue with God was conducted through Nathan—although David made his own contrite and repentant approach to God in Psalm 51. Again, when David numbered the people, God's judgement was communicated to David through the prophet Gad (2 Samuel 24:1-14).

God's Representatives

All down the ages, God has appointed representatives and intermediaries through whom He communicates with man, and through whom also man has access to Him, the Lord Jesus Christ being the perfect mediator between God and men.

But how was mediatorship first introduced in God's dealings with man? As always, we find the answer by turning back to Genesis and looking at the experiences of the patriarchs. These experiences lay the foundation of God's ways throughout the ages.

Consider Abraham. There are many examples of what appear to be prayers addressed directly to God:

"Abram said, Lord GOD, what wilt thou give me, seeing I go childless? … Lord GOD, whereby shall I know that I shall inherit it?" (15:2,8)

But on other occasions there is clearly an intermediary:

"Abraham stood yet before the LORD. And Abraham drew near, and said, Wilt thou also destroy the righteous with the wicked? Peradventure there be fifty righteous … Peradventure ten shall be found there. And he said, I will not destroy it for ten's sake." (18:22-32)

This was the time when Abraham pleaded with God on behalf of the righteous in Sodom, and particularly for Lot. Three "men" had appeared to Abraham; one of them—"the LORD"—stayed with Abraham, while "two angels" are referred to in the following chapter (19:1) as having arrived in Sodom. We are thus led to conclude that "the LORD" was a manifestation of God, His spokesman or messenger—an angel—in human form.

In a later passage, the occasion when Abraham prepares to slay Isaac, an angel is actually mentioned:

"And the angel of the LORD called unto him out of heaven, and said, Abraham, Abraham: and he said, Here am I. And he said, Lay not thine hand upon the lad … for now I know that thou fearest God." (22:11,12)

In some passages, therefore, it appears that Abraham spoke directly with God, but if Genesis 18 and 22 are a guide, then we can assume that, even when the patriarch appears to address God directly, it is in fact through an angel. It is no surprise to find in later instances that "angel" is used interchangeably with "God". For example:

"And *God spake* unto Israel in the visions of the night, and said, Jacob, Jacob ..."　　　　　　　　(Genesis 46:2)

"And *the angel of the LORD appeared* unto Moses ... out of the midst of a bush ..."　　　　　　　　(Exodus 3:2)

The Angel of God's Presence

We venture here into the exalted subject of God-manifestation. God chose to speak through angels, who were sent as His representatives. Frequently the record says that it was God who spoke, yet the context, and sometimes the actual wording, indicates that it was angels who brought His message.

Sometimes, there is reference to a particular angel: One who is sent as God's special emissary and who bears God's Name. In Exodus, Moses receives this assurance:

"Behold, *I send an Angel before thee*, to keep thee in the way ... Beware of him, and obey his voice, provoke him not; for he will not pardon your transgressions: for my name is in him ... *mine Angel shall go before thee*."
(Exodus 23:20,21,23; 32:34; 33:2)

Just as Abraham, the friend of God, spoke with the LORD and with His angel, so also did Moses: "The LORD spake unto Moses face to face, as a man speaketh unto his friend" (Exodus 33:11). Chapter 33, moreover, goes on to relate the conversation that Moses has with God, in which Moses, seeking reassurance, pleads, "Shew me now thy way ... that I may find grace in thy sight"; and the LORD then says, "*My presence* shall go with thee" (verses 13,14).

At first sight, this promise might seem to be saying that God would watch over His people in a general sense, but there is surely a more particular reference to the Angel of

God's presence—One who was given the great responsibility of bearing God's Name among the people of Israel, being His particular representative. And if this is not clear from Exodus, it is certainly evident from Isaiah 63. After enumerating the great attributes of the LORD—His lovingkindnesses, goodness and mercies (which are there too in Exodus 33 and 34)—the prophet writes:

> "In all their affliction he was afflicted, and *the angel of his presence* saved them: in his love, and in his pity he redeemed them; and he bare them, and carried them all the days of old." (Isaiah 63:7-9; cf. Acts 7:38)

Daniel received visitations from "the man Gabriel", an angel sent to reveal God's purpose in detailed visions (Daniel 8:16; 9:21). And centuries later Gabriel appeared to Zacharias and to Mary—once more with specific words of encouragement and instruction (Luke 1:19,26).

Moses and Aaron

There are other aspects of the work of angels which are very relevant to prayer, but we return now to the role of earthly mediators in the life of God's people. Reflecting on the passages we have reviewed so far, the conclusion we come to is that speaking with God, directly, or even through angels, was an experience mostly reserved for the more spiritually minded in Israel—people of the stature of Abraham, Moses, Hannah, David, Hezekiah or Daniel. What did the ordinary Israelite do? How did he or she pray?

Israel lived under the Law, and this provided arrangements for regular worship and ordinances for offerings—including peace offerings, thank offerings, and so on. But the Law plainly did not provide all that was required to fulfil man's need for prayer.

Many of the children of Israel were frankly afraid of manifestations of God. When, at Sinai, they "saw the thunderings, and the lightnings, and the voice of the trumpet ... they trembled, and stood afar off. And they said unto Moses, Speak thou with us, and we will hear: but let not

God speak with us, lest we die" (Exodus 20:18,19, RV; Deuteronomy 18:16; cf. 1 Samuel 12:19). In Aaron they had a high priest, and there was a comprehensive system of sacrifices and feasts, yet they felt the need for personal access to God. Thus Moses became a mediator—on the one hand, to convey God's word to the people, but also to represent their cause to Him. Mediatorship is thus a two-way process. Jethro described Moses' function in these words: "Be thou for the people to God-ward, that thou mayest bring the causes unto God" (Exodus 18:19).

After Moses, there were others who acted as mediators on behalf of a people who were often fearful to approach God themselves. Jeremiah was frequently asked to mediate: "Zedekiah the king sent ... to the prophet Jeremiah, saying, Pray now unto the LORD our God for us ..."—and the answer came back from God through the prophet (37:3-7; see also 42:1-7). Yet on at least three occasions God forbade the prophet: "Pray not thou for this people, neither lift up cry nor prayer for them, neither make intercession to me: for I will not hear thee" (7:16; 11:14; 14:11).

"A new and living way"

Our prayers are directed "through Jesus Christ our Lord". In referring to the mediatorship of the risen Lord, we are acknowledging his gracious work whereby we are redeemed and whereby we have access to the throne of grace. We now have "boldness to enter into the holiest by the blood of Jesus, by a new and living way" (Hebrews 10:19,20). There is more to be said on the subject of intercession in its New Testament context, but this will be reserved until chapter 15.

Of old Thy prophet Moses
Did for Thy people pray;
Appealed to Thee, Eternal,
And turned Thy wrath away.
Elijah's prayer Thou heardest
To close and open heaven;
O God, who heard the prophets,
To us Thy grace be given.

HYMN 238, VERSE 2

5

THE RICHNESS OF BIBLE WORDS

It should not surprise us that there are so many words connected with the topic of prayer. The large vocabulary reveals what enormous breadth of meaning this subject has and how important it was—and is—in the believer's life.

SO far, we have observed some of the ways in which the patriarchs and other great men of God learned to approach the Almighty in prayer, worship and sacrifice. We are beginning to define what prayer means—and already we are starting to realise what an immense subject

---

TABLE 1

BIBLE WORDS FOR PRAY / PRAYER

Ask	Order (my cause)
Beseech	Plead
Bow (the head)	Pour out (complaint)
Call upon	Praise
Commune	Pray
Cry	Seek
Draw near	Sing forth
Entreat	Spread forth (hands)
Fall down	Stretch out (hands)
Lift up (voice, hands)	Thank
Make supplication	Wait (upon)
Meditate	Worship

we have before us. Prayer may be personal meditation or public worship; it can be expressed in entreaty, in thanks, in exultation; in moments of sacred prayer the child of God may sigh, or beseech, or even keep silent—all this, and much more, is prayer. But how far does the definition extend?

The Vocabulary of Prayer

Let us attempt a brief survey of the vocabulary of prayer. We do not need an expert knowledge of Hebrew or Greek to discover that the Bible contains far more synonyms for prayer than we may at first have thought. But let us not start with Hebrew and Greek: let us first see how many English words there are which, in some sense, relate to our subject. Table 1 is a tentative list, and readers may think of others which could be added: these are all words which appear in the AV/KJV.

So the vocabulary of prayer is surprisingly large—far beyond the very limited and limiting definitions which perhaps initially come to mind. And this is the result of looking only at English words.

If now we refer to a concordance, we shall discover that our English words correspond to a large number of original words. For example, Young's tells us that where we have "beseech" in the AV, there are in fact five different Hebrew and two Greek words.

Hebrew Words

Twelve Old Testament words are translated in the AV by "pray" or "prayer" (in connection with God), each with its own subtle shade of meaning. The following are representative examples:

"Jonah prayed unto the LORD, and said, I pray (*ana*, Ah pray!) thee, O LORD ..." (Jonah 4:2)

"He shall pray (*athar*, to entreat, burn incense) unto God, and he will be favourable ..." (Job 33:26)

"Many people and strong nations shall come to seek ... and to pray (*chalah*, to entreat, be grieved) before the LORD ..." (Zechariah 8:22)

"If they bethink themselves ... and pray (*chanan*, entreat grace) unto thee in the land of their captivity ..." (2 Chronicles 6:37)

"LORD, in trouble have they visited thee, they poured out a prayer (*lachash*, sigh, whisper) ..." (Isaiah 26:16)

"What profit should we have, if we pray (*paga*, to meet, intercede) unto him?" (Job 21:15)

"Restore the man his wife; for he is a prophet, and he shall pray (*palal*, to ask another to intervene) for thee." (Genesis 20:7—first occurrence of "pray" in the Bible)

"Pray (*shaal*, to ask) for the peace of Jerusalem: they shall prosper that love thee." (Psalm 122:6)

"Evening, and morning, and at noon, will I pray (*siach*, to commune, meditate, complain), and cry aloud ..." (Psalm 55:17)

"Have mercy upon me, and hear my prayer (*tephillah*, prayer, song of praise)." (Psalm 4:1)

"Daniel ... prayed (*tsela*, to request, bow), and gave thanks before his God ..." (Daniel 6:10)

"Then these men assembled, and found Daniel praying (*ve'ah*, to petition, pray) and making supplication before his God." (Daniel 6:11)

New Testament Words

Turning now to the New Testament, there are five Greek words translated "pray" or "prayer" (three of them from the same root). The following are examples of each:

"Watch ye therefore, and pray (*deomai*, to want, pray, beseech) always ..." (Luke 21:36)

"I pray (*erotao*, to ask, interrogate) for them: I pray not for the world ..." (John 17:9)

"Pray (*euchomai*, to pray, wish) one for another, that ye may be healed ..." (James 5:16)

"Thinkest thou that I cannot now pray (*parakaleo*, to call for, or alongside) to my Father?" (Matthew 26:53)

"Pray (*proseuchomai*, to pray or wish for) for them which despitefully use you ..." (Matthew 5:44)

There is of course much more that could be said about these many different original words: their shades of meaning; the number of times each is used; and the fact that these same words may sometimes be translated, not by "pray" but by alternative English words. The above examples do, however, make us aware of the amazing variety of words connected with our subject.

Why Such a Rich Vocabulary?

It is a feature of all languages, that when people have a special interest or preoccupation, they extend their vocabulary to meet their needs. Today's obsessions with sport, cars and computers, for example, have spawned vast numbers of new words. And that can apply to spiritual preoccupations too. God's people in both Old and New Testament times had the privilege of divine instruction in the practice of prayer and, as a result, learned a wonderfully rich vocabulary of prayer—a wealth of words which has spilled over into our own mother tongue.

Lord, teach us how to pray aright,

With reverence and with fear;

Though dust and ashes in Thy sight,

We may, we must draw near.

HYMN 149, VERSE 1

6

"PRAISE YE THE LORD"

Worship is an essential part of prayer: we should be more ready to praise God, acknowledging His glory and majesty and hallowing His Name, than to pour out our own wants and sorrows. We may even bless God.

ONE of the twenty-four words listed in Table 1 (chapter 5) was "worship". This is such an important aspect of prayer that it deserves its own chapter. As mortal man approaches his Maker, the proper reaction is to acknowledge his own unworthiness and to bow in humble adoration of God's holiness and majesty. "Worship" is the declaration of God's 'worth-ship'. In fact, "worship" itself has so many aspects that we can draw up another table listing various Bible synonyms: see Table 2.

Each of the fourteen words in Table 2, if we think about it, proceeds from a distinct emotion in the one who prays. If

---

TABLE 2

BIBLE WORDS FOR WORSHIP

Bless	Honour
Bow the head	Magnify
Exalt	Praise
Extol	Rejoice in
Fear	Reverence
Glorify	Sanctify
Hallow	Worship

---

we *hallow* God's name, we are soberly acknowledging that God is set apart, holy, exalted beyond our human comprehension. If we *praise* the Almighty, we are extolling His great qualities, and this we do with rejoicing and song. *Fear* is different again: those who feared God were not so much afraid of Him but struck with awe and reverence as they bowed before Him in prayer.

Worship and Praise

Worship, in all its varied aspects, is evident in every book of the Bible. When Moses gave instructions for the first Passover, "the people *bowed the head* and *worshipped*" (Exodus 12:27). After Nebuchadnezzar had received the vision of the tree that was to be cut down, and had undergone the humiliation which the vision foretold, he wrote of his experiences: "Now I Nebuchadnezzar *praise* and *extol* and *honour* the King of heaven, all whose works are truth, and his ways judgment: and those that walk in pride he is able to abase" (Daniel 4:37). After receiving the angel's message, and also the blessing of Elisabeth, Mary the mother of Jesus said: "My soul doth *magnify* the Lord, and my spirit hath *rejoiced* in God my Saviour" (Luke 1:46,47).

Supremely, David and the other Psalmists poured out their worship and praise to God: "O LORD our Lord, how excellent is thy name in all the earth! who hast set thy glory above the heavens … " (Psalm 8:1). "Let every thing that hath breath praise the LORD. Praise ye the LORD" (150:6). Praise is a universal Bible theme.

Glory and Honour

Glory is one of God's attributes, seen in creation and in all God's works. As part of that creation we have the privilege of reflecting glory to God and giving Him honour, extolling Him for His majesty and power. Even though we have nothing that will add to the divine glory, God desires our worship and by that worship we glorify His Name:

"Give unto the LORD, O ye kindreds of the people, give unto the LORD glory and strength. Give unto the LORD the glory due unto his name: bring an offering, and come into his courts. O worship the LORD in the beauty of holiness: fear before him, all the earth." (Psalm 96:7-9)

In the Revelation, we read of the great acclamations of praise that will rise to God and to the Lamb in the kingdom age—for example:

"Every creature ... heard I saying, Blessing, and honour, and glory, and power, be unto him that sitteth upon the throne, and unto the Lamb for ever and ever."
(Revelation 5:13)

Meanwhile, God is glorified even now by those who come to Him through Christ, the one in whom was seen "the glory as of the only begotten of the Father, full of grace and truth" (John 1:14).

"Bless the LORD, O my soul"

One feature of praise that deserves mention is the idea of "blessing". We know, of course, that God blesses man: "God blessed them (the man and woman He had made), and God said unto them, Be fruitful and multiply ..." (Genesis 1:28). The person who is blessed of God receives God's favour. But the Scriptures speak frequently of man blessing God. Noah said: "Blessed be the LORD God of Shem" (9:26); and from the same era we have the words of Job: "The LORD gave, and the LORD hath taken away; blessed be the name of the LORD" (1:21). Moreover, in a passage about Abraham and Melchizedek, we read of man receiving God's blessing and God receiving man's blessing:

"Melchizedek ... blessed Abram, and said, *Blessed be Abram* of the most high God ... and *blessed be the most high God*, which hath delivered thine enemies into thy hand." (Genesis 14:19,20)

What exactly is intended when man says, "Blessed be God"? Often, it may be simply another way of saying "Praise be to God", or "Thanks be to God"—as, for example, in Moses' instructions to Israel: "When thou hast eaten and art full, then thou shalt bless the LORD thy God for the good land which he hath given thee" (Deuteronomy 8:10). But blessing is more than just the giving of thanks.

29

"Let us kneel before the LORD our Maker"

The Hebrew word *barak* comes from a root which means 'to kneel'. In the AV, it is usually translated "bless" or "blessed"—for example, "Sing unto the LORD, *bless* his name" (Psalm 96:2); but there are a couple of places where *barak* is rendered "kneel"—for example, "O come, let us worship and bow down; let us *kneel* before the LORD our maker" (Psalm 95:6). When man blesses God he is really saying that God is worthy to receive man kneeling before Him, offering humble worship. Though there is little we can do to magnify our Maker, yet by devotion and obedience we can give Him pleasure.

We now begin to see what is going through David's mind when he lifts up his voice to bless God, and calls on all creation to do the same:

"Bless the LORD, O my soul: and all that is within me, bless his holy name … Bless the LORD, all ye his works in all places of his dominion: bless the LORD, O my soul."
(Psalm 103:1,22)

Prayer and Blessing

In Old Testament times, the Levitical priests were the channel of communication between man and God, and one of the duties of Aaron and his sons was to bless the children of Israel using the priestly blessing:

"The LORD bless thee, and keep thee: the LORD make his face shine upon thee, and be gracious unto thee: the LORD lift up his countenance upon thee, and give thee peace."
(Numbers 6:24-26)

Blessing and prayer were complementary parts of priestly mediatorship. After the keeping of the passover in the time of Hezekiah, for example, we read of the priests blessing the people and bringing their prayers to God:

"The priests the Levites arose and *blessed* the people: and their voice was heard, and their *prayer* came up to his holy dwelling place, even unto heaven."
(2 Chronicles 30:27)

There were also spiritually minded kings like David and Solomon who at certain times led the people in a priestly role, blessing the nation and blessing God. When David had prepared all the materials for the building of the temple and commended to Israel Solomon his son—

"David said to all the congregation, Now *bless* the LORD your God. And all the congregation *blessed* the LORD God of their fathers, and bowed down their heads, and worshipped the LORD, and the king."

(1 Chronicles 29:20)

Another notable occasion was Solomon's dedication of the temple:

"When Solomon had made an end of praying all this prayer ... he stood, and *blessed all the congregation of Israel* with a loud voice, saying, *Blessed be the LORD*, that hath given rest unto his people ..."   (1 Kings 8:54-61)

Again, we see blessing as a two-way process: Solomon, having finished his long prayer of dedication, turned to bless the people—and at the same time blessed the LORD.

Blessing in the New Testament

In the New Testament, the practice of blessing continues. As a priest brought up in the Jewish tradition of prayer, Zacharias prophesied at the birth of John, saying, "Blessed be the Lord God of Israel; for he hath visited and redeemed his people" (Luke 1:68). Simeon took the infant Jesus in his arms "and blessed God" (2:28). After Christ's ascension, the disciples returned to Jerusalem "and were continually in the temple, praising and blessing God" (24:53).

Similar language is used, moreover, in the epistles: "Blessed be the God and Father of our Lord Jesus Christ, who hath blessed us with all spiritual blessings in heavenly places in Christ" (Ephesians 1:3; cf. Romans 1:25; 2 Corinthians 1:3; 1 Peter 1:3).

Jesus himself is the subject of blessing, when the multitudes (quoting Psalm 118:25,26) cry: "Hosanna to the Son of David: Blessed is he that cometh in the name of the

31

Lord" (Matthew 21:9; cf. 23:39). But the greatest acclamations of blessing are reserved for the day when thousands upon thousands sing: "Worthy is the Lamb that was slain to receive ... honour, and glory, and blessing"; and when angels and elders and living creatures fall on their faces and worship God, saying, "Blessing, and glory ... be unto our God for ever and ever. Amen" (Revelation 5:12; 7:11,12).

Can we bless God?

Blessing God was clearly a part of the language of prayer in Bible times. We may feel a certain inhibition in presuming to bless our Creator, but following the example of David and others, there is no reason why we should not commence a prayer with a phrase like "Blessed be Thou, Lord God ..." What is important is that by our worship, by our prayers, in the singing of our hymns, and in every aspect of our lives in Christ we give honour, glory, power and praise to Almighty God.

7

"SING UNTO THE LORD
A NEW SONG"

From the earliest times, music has enhanced man's worship and meditation. Believers sang of their joys and sorrows and Israel joined in congregational praise to God. We look forward to singing "a new song" in the age to come.

MUSIC is part of man's make-up: most people, even if they do not have the skill to sing or play themselves, at least appreciate the performance of music by others. Adding words to music, especially words of praise or petition to God, is surely the highest purpose to which this human endowment can be put. Though little trace remains of Hebrew music as it was in Bible times, we can imagine how beautiful it must have been.

Prayer, as we have seen, takes on many different forms and song is one of these forms. In the psalms, particularly, we see men of God worshipping and praising God in song, and we can picture David accompanying his words on the lyre or harp. On a much larger scale, the Levitical singers were accompanied by a range of orchestral instruments.

But songs of praise and supplication do not commence with the psalms: they have their origins farther back in the history of God's people. From the earliest times poetry formed part of the life of God's people. In Genesis we find, for example, the Song of Lamech (4:23,24) and the Blessings of Jacob (49:2-27). Much of the book of Job—including the Almighty's words to Job, and Job's faltering responses—is in poetic style.

"The LORD is my strength and song"

The Song of Moses, celebrating Israel's deliverance through the Red Sea, is a majestic song of praise, an expression of thankfulness and honour to God:

> "Then sang Moses and the children of Israel this song unto the LORD, and spake, saying, I will sing unto the LORD, for he hath triumphed gloriously: the horse and his rider hath he thrown into the sea. The LORD is my strength and song, and he is become my salvation ... Who is like unto thee, O LORD, among the gods? Who is like thee, glorious in holiness, fearful in praises, doing wonders?" (Exodus 15:1-18)

We assume that Moses taught the people this Song, which then became a pattern not just for great national songs but also doubtless for private prayers—certainly for those in Israel like Deborah, Hannah, David and others when they voiced their praise at important moments in the history of Israel or in their personal lives:

> "Then sang Deborah and Barak the son of Abinoam on that day, saying, Praise ye the LORD for the avenging of Israel, when the people willingly offered themselves. Hear, O ye kings; give ear, O ye princes; I, even I, will sing unto the LORD; I will sing praise to the LORD God of Israel ..." (Judges 5:1-31)

Hannah's Prayer

We refer to the Song of Hannah, but it is clearly a prayer, offered from a full and exultant heart to the God of Israel:

> "And Hannah prayed, and said, My heart rejoiceth in the LORD, mine horn is exalted in the LORD: my mouth is enlarged over mine enemies; because I rejoice in thy salvation ..." (1 Samuel 2:1-10)

Such, then, are some of the songs of Israel, even before we come to the psalms; and they were sung to the accompaniment of music in the idiom of the time—perhaps specially composed, or possibly (as some of the musical directions in the psalms suggest) using existing 'tunes' from Israel's heritage of music.*

David's reign introduced music and song on a much more elaborate scale, with organised choirs and full-time musicians. When the ark of the covenant was brought into its place in Jerusalem, David "spake to the chief of the Levites to appoint their brethren the singers, with instruments of music, psalteries and harps and cymbals, sounding aloud and lifting up the voice with joy" (1 Chronicles 15:16, RV).

The arrival of the ark in the city of David is then followed by further ceremonies involving the Levitical musicians and singers—"to thank and praise the LORD God of Israel" (1 Chronicles 16:4). It is interesting that the translation of verse 7 in the RSV and one or two other versions suggests that this was an innovation in the worship of Israel: "Then on that day David first appointed that thanksgiving be sung to the LORD by Asaph and his brethren". David, it seems, was here inaugurating the Levitical service of song. Singers and instrumentalists were being dedicated to a work which, though not concerned with sacrifices, was still essentially a priestly work: they had the serious and important task of leading the people of Israel in prayer and praise.

Asaph's song begins and ends as follows:

"Give thanks unto the LORD, call upon his name, make known his deeds among the people. Sing unto him, sing psalms unto him ...

O give thanks unto the LORD; for he is good; for his mercy endureth for ever. And say ye, Save us, O God of our salvation ... And all the people said, Amen, and praised the LORD." (1 Chronicles 16:8-36)

The office of Asaph and his musicians continued at least until the time of Hezekiah, "according to the command-

---

* Brother Mark Vincent's book, *Exploring the Psalms*, contains very helpful material on the poetry and music of Israel, and the psalms in particular.

ment of David, and of Gad the king's seer, and Nathan the prophet: for so was the commandment of the LORD ..." (2 Chronicles 29:25). The returning exiles, moreover, revived the music that was associated with the temple "after the ordinance of David king of Israel" (see Ezra 3:10,11; Nehemiah 12:27-46).

Personal and National Prayer

We naturally think of David as a man of personal prayer, yet he was clearly committed to making prayer an institution in the life of Israel. Even in a prayer as intensely personal as Psalm 22, there are sections where the psalmist (or the Messiah to whom he is looking) also embraces the people of Israel—and "all kindreds of the earth" who one day will share the opportunity to worship the God of Israel:

> "I will declare thy name unto my brethren: in the midst of the congregation will I praise thee. Ye that fear the LORD, praise him; all ye the seed of Jacob, glorify him ... All the ends of the world shall remember and turn unto the LORD: and all the kindreds of the nations shall worship before thee." (Psalm 22:22,23,27)

One final prayer of David is recorded before the end of his life. He "spake unto the LORD the words of this song in the day that the LORD had delivered him out of the hand of all his enemies, and out of the hand of Saul" (2 Samuel 22:1). It is part song, part prayer, as David reflects on what God has done for him, but also addresses God in thankfulness for all that he has been able to accomplish with His help.

The songs of Israel continue to be mentioned in the prophets. The phrase that we find in Psalm 33:3, 96:1 and 98:1—"Sing unto the LORD a new song"—is picked up by the prophet Isaiah (42:10). And when Amos records God's impatience with the worship of His people, he refers not just to the sacrifices but also to the music that had become part of the temple ritual: "Though ye offer me burnt offerings ... I will not accept them ... Take thou away from me the noise of thy songs; for I will not hear the melody of thy viols" (5:22,23). Looking to the end that was to come on

Israel, Amos adds: "The songs of the temple shall be howlings in that day, saith the Lord GOD" (8:3).

Mary's Song

But with the New Testament comes a very special new song. Echoing the prayer of Hannah, Mary's song rose to the throne of God in joyful acknowledgement of the favour bestowed on her:

> "My soul doth magnify the Lord, and my spirit hath rejoiced in God my Saviour ..." (Luke 1:46-55)

Finally, in the vision of the last things granted to John, the Old Testament idiom is used again:

> "They sung a new song, saying, Thou art worthy to take the book ... They sung as it were a new song before the throne ... And they sing the song of Moses the servant of God, and the song of the Lamb."
>
> (Revelation 5:9; 14:3; 15:3)

Those who one day hope to sing that new song can meanwhile enjoy the privilege of prayer and the singing of the Father's praises—"speaking one to another in psalms and hymns and spiritual songs, singing and making melody in your heart to the Lord" (Ephesians 5:19; Colossians 3:16).

O sing unto the LORD a new song:
  Sing unto the LORD, all the earth.
Sing unto the LORD, bless his name;
  Shew forth his salvation from day to day.
Declare his glory among the heathen,
  His wonders among all people.
For the LORD is great, and greatly to be praised:
  He is to be feared above all gods ...

Give unto the LORD, O ye kindreds of the people,
  Give unto the LORD glory and strength.
Give unto the LORD the glory due unto his name:
  Bring an offering, and come into his courts.
O worship the LORD in the beauty of holiness:
  Fear before him, all the earth.

PSALM 96:1-9 (1 CHRONICLES 16:23-30)

8

THE SWEET PSALMIST OF ISRAEL

In the Book of Psalms, David and others pour forth praises, laments, entreaties and confessions. Some psalms are reflective meditations; others celebrate God's mighty works. Many portray the sufferings and glory of the Messiah.

OUR brief review of the great songs of the Bible took us from Genesis to Revelation, but we really did not stop to give proper consideration to the psalms.

What is it about the psalms that is so special? They express, in the world's most beautiful words, the worship and yearnings of the true child of God. We may think of the

---

Types of Psalms

THE word "psalm" refers to a song, and comes from the Septuagint title of the book. The Hebrew name of the book is *Sepher Tehillim*, the Book of Praises. But not all the psalms are songs or praises: we encounter a range of different Hebrew words, including *tephillah*—prayer or entreaty (as in the headings of Psalms 17 and 90, and in 72:20); *mizmor*—a song of praise, usually with musical accompaniment (see titles of Psalms 3, 4, 5, 6 etc.); *shir*—a song (Psalms 30, 45, 120-134 etc.); *maschil*—a meditation, poem of instruction (Psalms 32, 42 etc.); *michtam*—a psalm of intense emotion (Psalm 16 etc.); and *shiggaion*—loud and bitter cry (Psalm 7; cf. Habakkuk 3:1).

*Brother Mark Vincent's book, **Exploring the Psalms**, contains valuable material for further study*

---

psalms as chiefly petitions or praise, but they also voice the believer's thanks, devotion, wonder, grief, melancholy, joy and exultation. When David, and other psalmists like Asaph, recorded the psalms, they wrote down all the concerns that they brought before their Maker—and that is why the psalms provide patterns of prayer and devotion for every child of God, in every situation. Jesus reflected constantly in the book of Psalms, and so should we.

Worship and Petition in the Psalms

A number of psalms are pure worship: the psalmist, forgetting his own cares, simply lifts up his voice in praise to God:

"O LORD our Lord, how excellent is thy name in all the earth! ... When I consider thy heavens, the work of thy fingers, the moon and the stars, which thou hast ordained; what is man, that thou art mindful of him? And the son of man, that thou visitest him? ... O LORD our Lord, how excellent is thy name in all the earth!"

(Psalm 8)

On the other hand, there are psalms which are pure petition. Psalm 51 we know as a penitential psalm, a cry for forgiveness after David's sin with Bathsheba. Chastened and repentant, he throws himself on God's mercy and lovingkindness. Yet the psalm is not wholly self-centred: its concluding verses have to do, not with David but with Zion:

"Have mercy upon me, O God, according to thy lovingkindness: according unto the multitude of thy tender mercies, blot out my transgressions ... For I acknowledge my transgressions: and my sin is ever before me ... Create in me a clean heart, O God; and renew a right spirit within me ... Do good in thy good pleasure unto Zion: build thou the walls of Jerusalem."   (Psalm 51)

We may not have sinned like David, and which of us in any case could express penitence as eloquently as David does? Yet this moving psalm is a pattern for any disciple bowed down with weakness, stricken with sin, but having faith that a gracious God will hear and forgive.

"The meditation of my heart"

Not all psalms, however, are pure worship or pure petition. Many combine the various elements of praise, supplications, reflection, vows—even imprecation (the calling down of judgement on one's enemies). Some, we might think, do not come into the category of prayers at all, being merely meditations. But is not meditation actually a form of communication with God?

By reading the psalms, we start to appreciate the vital interplay that exists between prayer and meditation. Meditation is the personal contemplation of God's being and purpose. It is part of the need we all have to "be still, and know that I am God" (Psalm 46:10). Meditation may simply be inward reflection, 'thinking one's own thoughts', but it can also spill over into prayer as the believer seeks to acknowledge in wonder and gratitude what God is and what He has done.

David's Experience

So interwoven and interchangeable are prayer and meditation in the psalmist's mind, that sometimes they alternate in the same verse:

> "The LORD lives! Blessed is my rock! Exalted be God, my deliverer ... For this I sing Your praise among the nations, LORD, and hymn Your name: He accords great victories to His king, keeps faith with His anointed, with David and his offspring forever."
> (Psalm 18:46-50, *Tanakh*, Jewish Publication Society)

Psalm 19 is another example: verses 1-6 contemplate God's majestic creation; verses 7-11, His law:

> "The heavens declare the glory of God; and the firmament sheweth his handywork ... The statutes of the LORD are right, rejoicing the heart: the commandment of the LORD is pure, enlightening the eyes ... " (verses 1-11)

As a shepherd David learned to know the close presence of the Almighty; in the silence of the hills, and under the canopy of the stars, he could marvel at God's mighty works.

But he also meditates on the fear of the LORD, and His righteous judgements, reflecting on what these things mean for himself—"by them is thy servant warned".

Such reflections lead David to seek God's help in resisting sin and remaining upright; and he concludes by asking that his words and meditation might be acceptable in God's sight:

> "Keep back thy servant also from presumptuous sins; let them not have dominion over me ... Let the words of my mouth, and the meditation of my heart, be acceptable in thy sight, O LORD, my strength, and my redeemer."
>
> (verses 13,14)

The way in which David offers, on the one hand, "the words of my mouth" and, on the other hand, "the meditation of my heart", makes it clear that, for him, both prayer and meditation were means of communication with the Almighty.

Messianic Psalms

Yet another feature of many of the psalms is prophecy, as David, by inspiration, sees beyond his own time to the appearing of the Suffering Servant, the coming of Israel's Messiah and ultimately the fulfilment of God's promises in the kingdom age:

> "Reproach hath broken my heart; and I am full of heaviness: and I looked for some to take pity, but there was none; and for comforters, but I found none. They gave me also gall for my meat; and in my thirst they gave me vinegar to drink." (Psalm 69:20,21)

> "Give the king thy judgements, O God, and thy righteousness unto the king's son ... His name shall endure for ever: his name shall be continued as long as the sun: and men shall be blessed in him: all nations shall call him blessed." (Psalm 72:1,17)

David's prayer and vision was of a world filled with justice and peace, when the poor and needy will be redeemed, and the whole earth will be full of God's glory. Our prayers should echo the same longings.

So many more aspects of the psalms could be considered; we could also look at 'psalm-prayers' in other books of Scripture—Hezekiah's (Isaiah 38:10-20); Habakkuk's (3:2-19); Jonah's (2:3-10) etc. This brief survey of praise, petition and meditation in the psalms will have to suffice.

Psalms and 'Ordinary' Prayers

This study may leave a question in some minds: Can God be approached more effectively by means of a song or a psalm than by an 'ordinary' prayer—in which case, what hope is there that God will hear our faltering and unpoetic prayers? Doubtless God took pleasure in the beauty of the psalms, but His response surely is not dependent on the form and eloquence of our words. Just as God looks not on the outward appearance in assessing human character, so He hears, not according to our skill with words but according to our fervour and sincerity of heart. David prayed in ordinary ways, as well as through his psalms. And there is no record that the Lord Jesus Christ, steeped though he was in the psalms, adopted a poetic style in prayer.

I waited patiently for the LORD;
> *He inclined to me and heard my cry.*
He drew me up from the pit of destruction,
>> *out of the miry bog,*
>> *And set my feet upon a rock,*
>> *making my steps secure.*
He put a new song in my mouth,
>> *a song of praise to our God.*
>> *Many will see and fear,*
>> *and put their trust in the LORD.*
Blessed is the man who makes the LORD his trust,
>> *Who does not turn to the proud,*
>> *to those who go astray after a lie!*
You have multiplied, O LORD my God, your won-
>> *drous deeds and your thoughts towards us;*
>> *None can compare with you!*
I will proclaim and tell of them,
>> *Yet they are more than can be told.*
Sacrifice and offering you have not desired,
>> *But you have given me an open ear.*
Burnt offering and sin offering you have not
>> *required.*
Then I said, 'Behold, I have come;
>> *In the scroll of the book it is written of me:*
I desire to do your will, O my God;
>> *Your law is within my heart.'*

PSALM 40:1-8, ESV

9

MEN AND WOMEN OF PRAYER

The faithful in Israel stood in awe of God, yet came close to Him in prayer: with Moses God spoke face to face. In the many examples of the pleadings of holy men and women of old we have patterns for our own prayers today.

WE have already mentioned a number of Old and New Testament characters whose prayers and songs are recorded for us, and we shall meet others later in the book. Many more examples of great men and women of prayer are to be discovered, however, and we shall look at a few of them now.

Moses

The meekest man in all the earth was a man of prayer. Of all God's servants, other than the Lord Jesus Christ, Moses was surely the one who was closest to God:

"And the LORD spake unto Moses face to face, as a man speaketh unto his friend."

(Exodus 33:11; Deuteronomy 34:10)

Time after time, Moses had to plead on behalf of a rebellious people. When Israel murmured at Rephidim, "Moses cried unto the LORD, saying, What shall I do unto this people? They be almost ready to stone me" (Exodus 17:4). But always he is humble: when Moses was in the mount to receive the tables of the Law, and the people sinned, Moses besought the LORD to forgive their sin—"and if not, blot me, I pray thee, out of thy book which thou hast written" (Exodus 32:11-13,31,32).

God heard Moses' pleas on behalf of Israel, but when Moses prayed for himself, that he might be allowed to enter the promised land, God refused:

"I besought the LORD at that time, saying, O Lord GOD, thou hast begun to shew thy servant thy greatness, and thy mighty hand: for what God is there in heaven or in earth, that can do according to thy works, and according to thy might? I pray thee, let me go over, and see the good land that is beyond Jordan ... But the LORD was wroth with me for your sakes, and would not hear me."
(Deuteronomy 3:23-26)

Samson, Elijah, Elisha

Samson was a man of faith, and evidently also a man of prayer. In his extremity, seeking to be avenged on the Philistines who had put out his eyes, he called unto God—and was heard:

"O Lord GOD, remember me, I pray thee, and strength-en me ... only this once, O God ..."   (Judges 16:28)

Elijah was a man of fervent prayer (James 5:16-18). When the son of the widow woman of Zarephath died, "he cried unto the LORD". But he did not sit and wait for the miracle to happen: he acted—"He stretched himself upon the child three times, and cried unto the LORD" (1 Kings 17:20,21). Elisha, in a similar way, raised the son of the Shunammite—by prayer, but also by action. These incidents remind us that our prayers, too, should be followed through by appropriate action. The healing of a person, or of a situation, is in the hand of God; but deeds of encouragement and kindness will work with our prayers to bring about His gracious response.

Hezekiah

When Hezekiah received the blasphemous letter from the king of Assyria, he "went up into the house of the LORD, and spread it before the LORD". This illustrates a golden rule in our relationship with God: lay the problem before Him, as Hezekiah did:

"And Hezekiah prayed before the LORD, and said, O LORD God of Israel ... bow down thine ear, and hear: open, LORD, thine eyes, and see: and hear the words of Sennacherib, which hath sent him to reproach the living God ... I beseech thee, save thou us out of his hand."

(2 Kings 19:14-19; Isaiah 37:15-20)

Note that Hezekiah was concerned first of all for the insult to the living God, and only secondly for the threat to God's people and to himself: that is an ordering of priorities for us to practise too. And the king was heard: for a while at least, Zion was safe; the angel of the Lord smote in the camp of the Assyrians 185,000 men; and Sennacherib was assassinated in the house of his god.

The following chapter records Hezekiah's more personal prayer: the king was ill, and Isaiah came with the message from God that he would die. The king might have concluded that there was no point in prayer—but the sick man turned weeping, with his face to the wall, and prayed:

"I beseech thee, O LORD, remember now how I have walked before thee in truth and with a perfect heart ..."

(2 Kings 20:1-3; Isaiah 38:1-3)

The answer came: "I have heard thy prayer, I have seen thy tears: behold, I will heal thee" (verse 5). Hezekiah, however, still wanted a sign that the Lord would heal him. God might have been provoked by this apparent reluctance to accept His word, but He met the request and brought back the shadow of the sundial ten degrees (2 Kings 20:8-11). Such was his faith, and such was God's mercy, that the king's prayer was heard and his life was lengthened.

Not every prayer for healing is heard—or rather, the prayer *is* heard but the answer may not always be the healing that we so desperately seek. We can only pray, in faith and fervour, and await God's will.

Jeremiah

The prayers—and lamentations—of Jeremiah reveal a man in touch with the Almighty, though still (like us) with much to learn. He acknowledges his own, as well as Judah's,

47

imperfections: "O LORD, I know that the way of man is not in himself: it is not in man that walketh to direct his steps. O LORD, correct me, but with judgment; not in thine anger, lest thou bring me to nothing" (Jeremiah 10:23,24); "O LORD, though our iniquities testify against us, do thou it for thy name's sake" (14:7,20,21). But it is from the court of the prison that Jeremiah's most eloquent prayer rises to his God:

> "Ah Lord GOD! behold, thou hast made the heaven and the earth by thy great power ... the Great, the Mighty God, the LORD of hosts, is his name ..." (32:16-24)

Nine of the ten verses of this prayer are ascriptions of praise to God, references to the signs and wonders which He wrought in the land of Egypt, and to the fact that the Chaldeans were now at the gates. Only in the tenth verse does Jeremiah come to the personal matter that was on his mind—the fact that in these dire circumstances God was commanding him to purchase a field in Anathoth:

> "... And thou hast said unto me, O Lord GOD, Buy thee the field for money, and take witnesses ..." (verse 25)

What an example for those of us who are so preoccupied with our wants and woes that we forget *first* to give honour to God. In contrast to Jeremiah, we are more likely to devote one-tenth of our prayer to Him and nine-tenths to ourselves!

Daniel

When Daniel "understood by books the number of the years, whereof the word of the LORD came to Jeremiah", he set his face unto the Lord God, "to seek by prayer and supplications, with fasting, and sackcloth, and ashes":

> "And I prayed unto the LORD my God, and made my confession, and said, O Lord, the great and dreadful God ... righteousness belongeth unto thee, but unto us confusion of faces, as at this day ... O Lord, hear; O Lord, forgive; O Lord, hearken and do; defer not, for thine own sake, O my God: for thy city and thy people are called by thy name." (Daniel 9:1-19)

There is in this prayer a rising intensity of supplication, as the prophet contrasts the righteousness of "the great and dreadful God" with the iniquity of His people, and the reproach that has come upon His city. The answer came swiftly, as Daniel feels the reassuring touch of Gabriel and receives the prophecy of the seventy weeks.

Ezra

The returning exiles were led by men of prayer. In particular, the company who set out with Ezra on the perilous journey to Jerusalem committed themselves early in the venture to God's safe-keeping. When they reached Ahava, it was time to stop and pray:

> "I proclaimed a fast there, at the river Ahava, that we might humble ourselves before our God, to seek from him a safe journey for ourselves ... For I was ashamed to ask the king for a band of soldiers and horsemen to protect us against the enemy on our way, since we had told the king, 'The hand of our God is for good on all who seek him ...' So we fasted and implored our God for this, and he listened to our entreaty." (Ezra 8:21-23, ESV)

On the frequent journeys that *we* make, how regularly do we stop and pray that God's hand will keep us and our little ones free from danger? How much do we really trust in our Father's providential care and in the angels who encamp round about them who fear Him (Psalm 34:7)? Do we thank God when we arrive home safe and sound?

Now safely at Jerusalem, Ezra has further cause for prayer when he discovers that the people had "mingled themselves with the people of the lands" (9:2). In a great confession similar to earlier ones from the lips of Jeremiah (14:20-22) and Daniel (9:3-19), and anticipating the prayer of the Levites in Nehemiah 9, Ezra fell upon his knees, spread out his hands to the LORD his God, and said:

> "O my God, I am ashamed and blush to lift up my face to thee, my God: for our iniquities are increased over our head, and our trespass is grown up unto the heavens ... we cannot stand before thee because of this." (9:6-15)

49

Nehemiah

Nehemiah was another paragon of prayer. Our minds go inevitably to that anxious time when he was challenged by King Artaxerxes regarding his sad countenance. What did he do? "I prayed to the God of heaven", he records (2:4). But though this might appear to be a prayer on impulse, Nehemiah was not a man who resorted to prayer only in a moment of panic: his was a life of regular prayer, and total commitment to God, as chapter 1 shows:

"When I heard these words, I sat down and wept, and mourned certain days, and fasted, and prayed before the God of heaven, and said, I beseech thee, O LORD, the God of heaven, the great and terrible God ... let thine ear now be attentive ... while I confess the sins of the children of Israel ... and prosper, I pray thee, thy servant this day, and grant him mercy in the sight of this man. (Now I was cupbearer to the king.)" (1:4-11,RV)

Nehemiah had been praying "day and night" for several months (from Chisleu, the ninth month, to Nisan, the first month of the new year—see 1:1 and 2:1) before he stood in the presence of the king. All that Nehemiah did was rooted in the habit of prayer. And throughout his book, as he writes of the events that led to the restoration of the city and its religious life, he punctuates his account with little 'asides' which reveal a man constantly in prayer to God:

"Hear, O our God; for we are despised." (4:4)

"Think upon me, my God, for good." (5:19)

"Now therefore, O God, strengthen my hands." (6:9)

"Remember me, O my God, concerning this, and wipe not out my good deeds ... Remember me, O my God, concerning this also, and spare me ... Remember me, O my God, for good." (13:14,22,31)

The lesson of Nehemiah is that at every turn in life, in every situation, whatever grief or joy or challenge lies in our path, we speak to God: He is our confidant; from Him we seek direction, reassurance, comfort, strength.

Zacharias, Mary ...

When we turn to the New Testament, the principles are the same, and the language of prayer is virtually the same, even if what is recorded is now in Greek. Jews continue to pray in Old Testament forms, and God continues to reveal His will through visions, dreams and angelic visitation. The divine appearances to Zacharias (Luke 1:11-20), Mary (1:26-37), Joseph (Matthew 1:20,21; 2:13 etc.), and the shepherds (Luke 2:9-14) could have been straight out of Genesis or Judges; and the responses of Mary, of Zacharias, of Simeon and others were typically the responses of the faithful in any age.

Simeon and Anna

Simeon, taking the infant Jesus in his arms, "blessed God, and said, Lord, now lettest thou thy servant depart in peace, according to thy word: for mine eyes have seen thy salvation ..." (Luke 2:28-32). Anna, a devout woman, "departed not from the temple, but served God with fastings and prayers night and day ... She coming in that instant gave thanks likewise unto the Lord, and spake of him to all them that looked for redemption in Jerusalem" (2:37,38).

The Gospels introduce us to people who were attentive to God's word, and who worshipped and prayed just as their forefathers did. When Zacharias received the angelic visitation, "the whole multitude ... were praying without at the time of incense" (Luke 1:10)—and we assume their prayers were sincere. Not all were like that, of course: Jesus condemned the hypocrites who "love to pray standing in the synagogues and in the corners of the streets, that they may be seen of men"; who use "vain repetitions ... for they think that they shall be heard for their much speaking" (Matthew 6:5-7) and who "for a pretence make long prayers" (Mark 12:40). Those who should have known better had strayed from the true path of prayer, and Jesus had to instruct his disciples anew in the art of approach to God:

"But thou, when thou prayest, enter into thine inner chamber, and having shut thy door, pray to thy Father which is in secret, and thy Father which seeth in secret shall recompense thee." (Matthew 6:6, RV)

The Lord may have had Daniel in mind: "When Daniel knew that the writing was signed, he went into his house; and his windows being open in his chamber toward Jerusalem, he kneeled upon his knees three times a day, and prayed, and gave thanks before his God" (6:10). Knowing of his habits, Daniel's adversaries found him "praying and making supplication before his God" (6:11). That is the habit of prayer which Jesus taught his disciples—and us.

Stephen

Later chapters will deal with the prayers of the Lord Jesus, the prayers of the first century ecclesias, and prayers in the epistles—including those of Paul. The apostles had learned from their Lord how to pray, and this becomes evident in the few words recorded of Stephen's prayer, which so closely echo the last words of the Lord himself:

"He, being full of the Holy Spirit, looked up stedfastly into heaven, and saw the glory of God, and Jesus standing on the right hand of God ... And they stoned Stephen, calling upon the Lord, and saying, Lord Jesus, receive my spirit. And he kneeled down, and cried with a loud voice, Lord, lay not this sin to their charge."

(Acts 7:55-60, RV)

Note the unique experience that Stephen is granted, being, as it were, lifted into heavenly places to behold the glory of God, and Jesus his intercessor at God's right hand: the very experience was a parable of prayer. Jesus graciously receives Stephen's words of committal and brings them into the presence of God.

In so few words, Stephen says so much: he acknowledges the supremacy of God and the role of the risen Christ; he commits himself to his Lord; and he asks forgiveness for those who had brought about his death—including Saul, by whose conversion the work which Stephen began would be continued.

10

"HE THAT COMETH TO GOD ..."

God is ready to bless us abundantly, but we cannot expect Him to help if unconfessed sin stands in the way. If, however, we confess and seek forgiveness; if our prayers are fervent, persistent, and according to His will, He will hear.

THOSE who come to God in prayer come with a spontaneous desire to worship their Maker: we were made to respond to the majesty and love of God. We come with a deep sense of need, acknowledging our unworthiness and the great privilege of access that has been granted us. So with these two driving forces — our desire and our need — what can possibly stand in the way of prayer?

Preconditions for Prayer

Does God set conditions for prayer? Can we assume that He will always listen to us? Of course God knows everything: He knows all that we are saying or thinking. But the fact that God knows is not the same as saying that He *hears* our cry. Scripture records a number of occasions when God would not listen to His people; when even the priests and prophets of God could not make their representations to Him:

> "Pray not thou for this people, neither lift up a cry or prayer for them: for *I will not hear them* in the time that they cry unto me for their trouble."
>
> (Jeremiah 11:14; cf. 7:16; 14:11)

Why would God not hear? The answer is there in the same chapter:

"They refused to hear my words ... the house of Israel and the house of Judah have broken my covenant ... though they shall cry unto me, I will not hearken unto them." (11:10,11)

Proverbs contains a similar declaration:

"Then shall they call upon me, but I will not answer; they shall seek me early, but they shall not find me." (Proverbs 1:28)

The reason, again, is that those who should have followed Wisdom's ways refused to listen:

"I have called, and ye refused; I have stretched out my hand, and no man regarded ... they hated knowledge, and did not choose the fear of the LORD." (1:24,29)

The fact that God's people kept the Law was no guarantee that they sought the LORD with a true heart:

"Your new moons and your appointed feasts my soul hateth ... And when ye spread forth your hands, I will hide mine eyes from you: yea, when ye make many prayers, I will not hear ... Wash you, make you clean; put away the evil of your doings from before mine eyes." (Isaiah 1:14-16)

"Your sins have hid his face from you"

And at the end of Isaiah, the rebuke is repeated, emphasising once more that sin separates man from God and prevents Him from hearing prayer:

"Behold, the LORD's hand is not shortened, that it cannot save; neither his ear heavy, that it cannot hear: but your iniquities have separated between you and your God, and your sins have hid his face from you, that he will not hear." (59:1,2)

But can we not argue that in Christ the barriers have been removed, through baptism our sin is purged, and God will no longer hide His face from us? Later in the same chapter Isaiah goes on: "He saw that there was no man, and wondered that there was no intercessor: therefore his own arm brought salvation ..." (verse 16,RV). It is true that in Christ we are accounted righteous. Yet unconfessed sin can still separate us from our Father: if we refuse to acknowledge our fault, and do not seek forgiveness, there is still an obstacle in the way of our communication with Him.

"Ye ask amiss"

James is very forthright in identifying why his readers do not receive answers to their prayers:

"Ye lust, and have not ... ye fight and war, yet ye have not, because ye ask not. Ye ask, and receive not, because ye ask amiss, that ye may consume it upon your lusts."

(James 4:2,3)

This is strong language, but it is clear from this and other passages that we cannot expect God to grant us special favours while we continue unrepentant in sin. God will not hear us: even though we come in the name of our Lord Jesus Christ, if we do not approach in a repentant spirit, we cannot expect our petitions to be granted.

"To this man will I look"

What other preconditions apply to our prayers? We should of course come before God in humility and contrition:

"To this man will I look, even to him that is poor and of a contrite spirit, and trembleth at my word."

(Isaiah 66:2)

Jesus taught the same principle in his parable of the Pharisee and the tax collector:

"The Pharisee stood and prayed thus with himself, God, I thank thee, that I am not as other men are ... And the publican, standing afar off, would not lift up so much as his eyes unto heaven, but smote upon his breast, saying, God be merciful to me a sinner. I tell you, this man went down to his house justified rather than the other."

(Luke 18:10-14)

The Pharisee prayed, not with God, but "with himself": his were empty, self-flattering words and the one who

55

uttered them failed in that basic requirement of contrition before the Almighty. The prayer of the publican, on the other hand, was the humble outpouring of a man who was aware of his unworthiness and threw himself upon God's mercy. Incidentally, his seven words—"God be merciful to me a sinner"—form an admirable pattern prayer for all sinners in all circumstances: it does not say everything, but as a simple and sincere petition, it says enough.

Those who would seek the Father's blessing and an answer to their prayers, should have a zeal for God's word; a delight in Scripture as the source of instruction from which they draw daily and by which their lives are sustained. *Can we truly expect God to listen to us, if we do not listen to the message of His Word?* Reading our Bibles we shall in fact, time and again, find the answer to life's questions; and while God can provide guidance in many and varied ways, the clear and obvious way in which He sheds light upon our path is through our reading of His word.

"Let him ask in faith"

Faith is also a vital precondition. With faith, said Jesus, mountains can be moved; in fact, "whatsoever ye shall ask in prayer, *believing*, ye shall receive" (Matthew 21:22). "He that cometh to God must believe that he is, and that he is a rewarder of them that diligently seek him" (Hebrews 11:6). Our faith is often weak; we struggle to believe that the impossible is possible with God. James vigorously condemns those who lack faith—a shortcoming that we might consider less grievous than outright transgression:

> "If any of you lack wisdom, let him ask of God … But let him ask in faith, nothing wavering. For he that wavereth is like a wave of the sea driven with the wind and tossed. For let not that man think that he shall receive any thing of the Lord." (James 1:5-7)

We would prefer James to be a bit milder in tone, yet this is what the Scripture says: God will graciously hear us, and gladly answer us—but not if unrepented sin, or faithlessness, stands in the way.

On the other hand, there are scriptures which encourage us to have boldness as we approach the throne of grace:

"In Christ Jesus we have boldness and access in confidence through our faith in him."

(Ephesians 3:12, RV; cf. Hebrews 4:16; 10:19)

"This is the confidence that we have in him, that, if we ask any thing according to his will, he heareth us: and if we know that he hear us, whatsoever we ask, we know that we have the petitions that we desired of him."

(1 John 5:14,15)

If we have faith, then, we may assuredly have confidence to come before our God in prayer. But how do we ask "according to his will"? Often, the point of our prayer is to try to discover His will. Does it not mean, that we seek by our prayers those objects which (so far as we can judge) are in accordance with God's purpose, and which will give Him glory? Even then, because we can never be completely certain which outcome will be "according to his will", we add the qualification "God willing", or "If the Lord will". Like our Master, we say, "Thy will be done".

Persistence

There are other prerequisites for prayer: we should be fervent (James 5:16); unselfish, giving more attention to praising God and honouring His Son than to our own desires. We should be thankful; and we should approach God's presence with joy. And one characteristic of prayer that is specially commended in Scripture is persistence.

We think of Abraham pleading for Sodom. Genesis 18 actually records a series of brief prayers, each more urgent than the one before it, in which Abraham intercedes on behalf of the few righteous that there may be in Sodom, including Lot and his family. This is how Abraham's six successive prayers address the Lord:

"And Abraham drew near, and said, Wilt thou also destroy the righteous with the wicked? Peradventure ..."

"And Abraham answered and said, Behold now, I have taken upon me to speak unto the LORD, which am but dust and ashes: Peradventure ..."

"And he spake unto him yet again, and said, Peradventure ..."

"And he said unto him, Oh let not the Lord be angry, and I will speak: Peradventure ..."

"And he said, Behold now, I have taken upon me to speak unto the Lord: Peradventure ..."

"And he said, Oh, let not the Lord be angry, and I will speak yet but this once: Peradventure ..." (verses 23-32)

What can we learn from Abraham's manner of approach? Notice that the prayers were intense, yet humble; they were preoccupied with one matter only—they did not offer praise or beseech forgiveness. We might feel that they were incomplete or inadequate prayers, yet Abraham was in no way chided; and though Sodom was not saved, the LORD was merciful to Lot and his family. God saw the faith and sincerity of the one who prayed.

Isaiah teaches us the virtue of persistence in prayer:

"On your walls, O Jerusalem, I have set watchmen; all the day and all the night they shall never be silent. You who put the LORD in remembrance, take no rest, and give him no rest until he establishes Jerusalem and makes it a praise in the earth." (Isaiah 62:6,7, ESV)

And the Lord Jesus taught the same lesson in his parables of the householder and the importunate widow:

"Though he will not get up and give him anything because he is his friend, yet because of his impudence he will ... give him whatever he needs." (Luke 11:8, ESV)

"And will not God give justice to his elect, who cry to him day and night?" (18:7, ESV)

The barriers are of our own making; God delights in the worship and prayers of His children.

11

THE MASTER AT PRAYER

Jesus gained strength and instruction from constant prayer to his Father. He prayed at critical moments in his ministry; he prayed at the Last Supper, in Gethsemane, and on the cross. He prayed for his disciples — and for us.

NONE of us can pray as Jesus prayed. Though we are given glimpses of the Son of God in prayer, we do not know all that he said in the long hours of intense communion with his Father. We can imagine our Lord, when the crowds dispersed, retreating into the inner chamber — or to the hills — to speak with God:

"And in the morning, rising up a great while before day, he went out, and departed into a solitary place, and there prayed."
(Mark 1:35)

"And when he had sent the multitudes away, he went up into a mountain apart to pray: and when the evening was come, he was there alone." (Matthew 14:23)

And God would answer: these were times when God revealed to the Son what he should declare to the world and to his disciples: "I speak to the world those things that I have heard of him" (John 8:26,40); "All things that I have heard of my Father I have made known unto you" (15:15).

The Man of Prayer

We find him at prayer especially when he was about to enter on a critical phase of his ministry. He prayed at the time of his own baptism:

> "Jesus, also being baptized, and praying ... the Holy Spirit descended ... and a voice came from heaven, which said, Thou art my beloved Son; in thee I am well pleased."   (Luke 3:21,22)

Later, faced with the clamour of the people, and aware of his growing fame, Jesus again sought strength in prayer:

> "And he withdrew himself into the wilderness, and prayed."   (5:16)

The night before he was to choose the Twelve, a matter for which he particularly needed insight and blessing—

> "He went out into a mountain to pray, and continued all night in prayer to God. And when it was day, he called unto him his disciples: and ... chose twelve ..."   (6:12,13)

Luke's Emphasis on Prayer

It is Luke who, more than the other evangelists, emphasises the role of prayer in the life of the Master. For example, while Matthew, Mark and Luke all record the confession at Caesarea Philippi, only Luke introduces his account with a reference to the Lord at prayer:

> "And it came to pass, as he was alone praying, his disciples were with him: and he asked them, saying, Whom say the people that I am?"   (9:18; see also 11:1)

Notice the paradox: Jesus is alone, yet with his disciples! He might well have preferred complete solitude, to be alone with his Father—but for the disciples' sake he shared with them those precious moments of intimacy with God.

It was the same on the occasion of the transfiguration. Matthew and Mark overlook the fact that this took place as the Lord was at prayer, but here are Luke's words:

> "... he took with him Peter and John and James, and went up into the mountain to pray. And as he was praying, the fashion of his countenance was altered ..."
> (9:28,29, RV)

In the sense that prayer is the meeting and communing of man with God, the whole experience of the transfiguration was one of prayer. Just as Moses met God in the Mount, spoke with Him, and received the revelation of His attributes, descending with the tables of the testimony, his face shining (Exodus 34), so Jesus as he prayed was transfigured, and the privileged three saw his glory. Moreover, as at the Lord's baptism, the Father's voice sounded out, saying, "This is my beloved Son: hear him" (Luke 9:35).

When the seventy returned from their mission, Jesus rejoiced in spirit, and prayed:

> "I thank thee, O Father, Lord of heaven and earth, that thou hast hid these things from the wise and prudent, and hast revealed them unto babes: even so, Father; for so it seemed good in thy sight."   (Luke 10:21)

When he was about to manifest his Father's power by raising Lazarus, he said:

> "Father, I thank thee that thou hast heard me. And I knew that thou hearest me always: but because of the people which stand by I said it, that they may believe that thou hast sent me."   (John 11:41,42)

"Now is my soul troubled"

And as his hour drew near, he prayed the more fervently to his Father:

> "Now is my soul troubled; and what shall I say? Father, save me from this hour: but for this cause came I unto this hour. Father, glorify thy name." (John 12:27,28)

In Gethsemane, the Saviour was "exceeding sorrowful, even unto death" and three times, leaving Peter, James and John to slumber, he withdrew and prayed:

> "He kneeled down, and prayed, saying, Father, if thou be willing, remove this cup from me: nevertheless not my will, but thine, be done ... And being in an agony he prayed more earnestly ..."   (Luke 22:41-44)

His "supplications with strong crying and tears" (Hebrews 5:7) were heard, and "there appeared an angel unto him from heaven, strengthening him" (Luke 22:43).

On the cross, he first prayed for his tormentors: "Father, forgive them; for they know not what they do". Then, about the ninth hour—and with Psalm 22 impressing itself on his mind—he cried with a loud voice, "My God, my God, why hast thou forsaken me?" (Matthew 27:46). Finally, with a last quotation from the psalms, the Son of God committed himself to the Father who indeed had not forsaken him: "Father, into thy hands I commend my spirit" (Luke 23:46; Psalm 31:5).

"Holy Father ..."

There is one prayer we have overlooked. We return to John 17 where we are granted the amazing privilege of listening in, as it were, to the confiding of the Son with his Father:

> "Father, the hour is come; glorify thy Son, that thy Son also may glorify thee ..."   (verses 1-5)

He continues then in prayer for his disciples:

> "I have manifested thy name unto the men which thou gavest me out of the world ... I pray for them ... Holy Father, keep through thine own name those whom thou hast given me, that they may be one, as we are ... I pray not that thou shouldest take them out of the world, but ... keep them from the evil."   (verses 6-19)

And in conclusion, the Lord petitions his Father on behalf of all believers—ourselves included:

> "Neither pray I for these alone, but for them also which shall believe on me through their word; that they all may be one; as thou, Father, art in me, and I in thee, that they also may be one in us ..."   (verses 20-26)

As Jesus prayed for Peter—"that thy faith fail not" (Luke 22:32)—so he prayed for all his disciples; and this great prayer, uniquely recorded by John, assures us that he also prays for us.

12

THE LORD'S PRAYER

The Lord Jesus gave his disciples this pattern for their prayers: a concise yet comprehensive summary of all that we need to bring before our Heavenly Father; the basis of more elaborate personal or communal petitions to God.

IN his Sermon on the Mount, Jesus introduced his disciples to a new way of thinking. They had been brought up under the Law, and though the Law was "holy, and just, and good", it had been overlaid with Pharisaic attitudes. Jesus had come to do away with a system that could never reconcile man and God. "Ye have heard that it was said ..." must now give way to, "But I say unto you ..."

The Lord's Prayer was given in that context: "When thou prayest, thou shalt not be as the hypocrites are ... After this manner therefore pray ye ..." (Matthew 6:5-9). Then follows the pattern prayer that Jesus taught (verses 9-13).

Model Prayers

Luke records a shorter form of the Prayer given on a later occasion. The context then was the request by one of Jesus' disciples, that he should teach them to pray "as John also taught his disciples" (Luke 11:1). Rabbis would teach their disciples model prayers, in particular 'fountain' prayers — shorter alternatives to the longer, more formal synagogue prayers of the time. John the Baptist had evidently done something along these lines, and it was natural that Jesus' disciples should expect him to follow the same tradition. Thus Luke records his version of the Prayer (Luke 11:2-4).

It shows slight variations from Matthew and omits the concluding doxology, but it is in essence the same prayer.*

What was the purpose of the Lord's Prayer? Jesus clearly wanted to encourage his disciples in their desire to pray, but using his suggested pattern rather than imitating the elaborate wordiness that was the fashion of the time. The disciples did not necessarily use the prayer as it stood, but developed it as a framework for fuller prayers—as we do.

"Our Father ... in heaven"

The Lord's Prayer in many respects broke new ground. On the other hand, there are numerous echoes of the Old Testament in both its style and content. Jesus surely must have had in mind David's prayer for Solomon:

> "*Blessed be thou*, LORD God of Israel *our father, for ever and ever*. Thine, O LORD, is the greatness, and *the power, and the glory* ... for all that is *in the heaven and in the earth* is thine; *thine is the kingdom*, O LORD, and thou art exalted as head over all ... We thank thee, and praise thy glorious *name* ..."   (1 Chronicles 29:10-13)

The title "Father" is also to be found in a number of other significant Old Testament passages:

> "Doubtless thou art *our father* ... thou, O LORD, art *our father*, our redeemer; thy name is from everlasting."
> (Isaiah 63:16; cf. 64:8; Deuteronomy 32:6; Psalm 103:13)

Why does the Prayer begin "*Our* Father"? Why not—'*My* Father, which art in heaven ...'? ("I", "me", and "my" do not

---

*Several phrases of the Prayer, in both Matthew and Luke, are omitted in many modern Bible versions, which claim to follow more reliable original Greek manuscripts. Not all experts, however, are convinced that the omissions, here and in other places in the Gospels and Acts, are justified. Brother John Carter, in connection with an RV omission in John 5, quotes the conclusion of A. C. Clark in his book *The Primitive Text of the Gospels and Acts:* "The primitive text is the longest, not the shortest" (*The Gospel of John*, ch. 5). We shall assume that the fuller versions of the Lord's Prayer are authentic.

occur in the Lord's Prayer; only "we", "us" and "our".) One answer is that "Our" reflects the fellowship of those who as members of a community pray to God. But there is a deeper reason for the use of "Our". For Jesus, God was "my Father" in a literal and intimate sense. For us, God is "Father" when, by belief and baptism into Christ, we are "born of God" and become adopted sons and daughters. There is a difference, therefore, between Jesus' sonship and ours, a difference which he himself made clear when he said to his disciples: "I ascend to *my* Father, and *your* Father; and to *my* God, and *your* God" (John 20:17).

Although in our Greek New Testament, *pater* is the word for Father, *Abba* would have been the word used when Jesus gave the prayer to his Aramaic-speaking disciples. Abba indeed occurs several times in the New Testament:

> "Abba, Father, all things are possible unto thee; take away this cup from me: nevertheless not what I will, but what thou wilt." (Mark 14:36)

> "Ye have received the Spirit of adoption, whereby we cry, Abba, Father ..." (Romans 8:15; cf. Galatians 4:6)

It has been suggested that where "Abba" occurs in Romans and Galatians, Paul may be referring, not just to disciples calling upon the Father, but to the actual praying of the Lord's Prayer by those who are sons by adoption. In Jewish literature, a writing was often cited by its first word—and in Aramaic the first word of the Lord's Prayer was Abba.

"Abba" was an intimate way of addressing a father, but this must not encourage us to bring the Father down to our level. The words "in heaven" remind us of the exaltedness and holiness of God: "God is in heaven, and thou upon earth: therefore let thy words be few" (Ecclesiastes 5:2). And God Himself reminds us that "as the heavens are higher than the earth, so are my ways higher than your ways, and my thoughts than your thoughts" (Isaiah 55:9).

"Hallowed be thy name"

In the English translation we miss the energy and vigour which was there originally in the first three petitions of the

Prayer: "*Hallowed* be thy name; *come* thy kingdom; *done* be thy will"—urgent, direct and yet simple petitions.

The reference to the Father's exaltedness in heaven leads on to the second phrase of the Prayer: "Hallowed be thy name". God's name is of course already hallowed: whether or not we pray this prayer, God is and always will be holy. He is "the Holy One"; and though His holiness in one sense separates Him from His creation, it is a quality which actually draws Him to His people. He desires to be sanctified, glorified, hallowed by those who serve Him.

When Nadab and Abihu died before the LORD for offering "strange fire", Moses reported God's pronouncement: "I will be sanctified in them that come nigh me, and before all the people I will be glorified" (Leviticus 10:3). Those who do not hallow God's Name are in danger of blaspheming it, as Paul warns the Romans: "For the name of God is blasphemed among the Gentiles because of you" (Romans 2:24,RV).

We hallow God's Name by our worship and praise, but also by all that we do in lives of service to Him: "Let your light so shine before men, that they may see your good works, *and glorify your Father which is in heaven*" (Matthew 5:16). And those who hallow God's name will themselves be changed in the process—another truth to be found in Leviticus: "Neither shall ye profane my holy name; but I will be hallowed among the children of Israel: I am the LORD *which hallow you*" (22:32).

When we say, "Hallowed be thy name", we are therefore, first, acknowledging God's holiness; second, seeking to make known God's holiness; and third, striving to manifest that holiness in our own lives. Our Lord did all of these; and in recognition of what he accomplished we are called upon not only to hallow the Father's name, but to "sanctify in your hearts *Christ* as Lord" (1 Peter 3:15, RV)—or, "in your hearts regard Christ the Lord as holy" (ESV).

"Thy kingdom come"

The kingdom of God, His sovereignty and kingship, are once again no new concepts: they were the bedrock of the purpose of God from ancient times: "The LORD reigneth ... Thy throne is established of old" (Psalm 93:1,2). "The LORD hath prepared his throne in the heavens; and his kingdom ruleth over all" (103:19; cf. 145:11-13).

When we pray, "Thy kingdom come", this is not merely a request that God should hasten His purpose, send His Son, and set up the kingdom; it is at the same time the expression of our hope to be granted a place in that kingdom. It is also a recognition that we should be proclaiming that kingdom, and *even now* living according to its principles.

"Thy will be done"

In this phrase we beseech the Father to fulfil His purpose, to consummate His will for the earth and for mankind: "In love he predestined us for adoption through Jesus Christ, according to the purpose of his *will* ... a plan for the fullness of time, to unite all things in him, things *in heaven* and things *on earth*" (Ephesians 1:4-10, ESV).

Yet again, however, our plea is not just for the fulfilment of that ultimate ideal but an acknowledgement that God's will is to be sought in the conduct of our present lives. In Gethsemane, the Lord Jesus prayed, "Thy will be done" (Matthew 26:39,42), in faith that his Father was in control. We too commit ourselves to God's will. However much we might desire a particular answer, God—for our good—may decree otherwise. Sometimes, we are more inclined to plead, 'Thy will be changed' than "Thy will be done"!

"As in heaven, so on earth"

So end the first three God-directed petitions of the Lord's Prayer. Then comes the phrase "in earth as it is in heaven". We usually associate this with "Thy will be done" but authorities assure us that it qualifies all that precedes it: the hallowing of God's name; the coming of His kingdom; and the fulfilment of His will. The two references to heaven are thus linked together: 'Our Father *in heaven* ... may Thy Name be hallowed, Thy sovereignty extended, and Thy will be done, on earth as they are *in heaven*.'

"Give us this day our daily bread"

The three God-ward petitions are followed by three concerned with ourselves, and in every prayer this must surely be the order of priority: God first; ourselves second.

The Greek word translated "daily bread" (RV margin, "bread for the coming day") appears to be the word used for the ration given to slaves and soldiers—and often allocated the day before. The idea is that we should ask God simply to supply sufficient daily food for tomorrow; and the idea (though not the same word) is there, too, in the parable of "the faithful and wise steward, whom his lord shall set over his household, to give them *their portion of food* in due season" (Luke 12:42,RV).

Everything about the prayer for daily bread takes us back to the provision of the manna in the wilderness:

> "Behold, I will rain bread from heaven … the people shall go out and gather *a certain rate every day* (or, a day's portion every day, RV, ESV)."   (Exodus 16:4)

There is, in fact, an additional possibility: that "bread for the coming day" may refer to the extra allocation of manna which God gave Israel on the sixth day to provide for the sabbath. And is there not a spiritual type here? When we ask for the provision of our "bread for the coming day", we are asking God to grant the sustenance—not just temporal food, but the bread of life—that will keep us until the great day of rest which is to come.

As far as our daily food is concerned, we are seeking sufficient, not excess; we are trusting God to relieve us of the worry as to where our next meal is coming from:

> "Remove far from me vanity and lies: give me neither poverty nor riches; feed me with the *food that is needful* for me."   (Proverbs 30:8,RV)

For the millions who suffer starvation in the world today, the prayer is acute and real. For those who have an abundance, the prayer may have a hollow ring: they should then at least pray for those who do not have enough.

"Forgive us our debts, as we forgive our debtors"

Matthew has "debts"; Luke has "sins"; while Matthew, in the two verses which follow the Prayer, speaks of "trespasses" (Matthew 6:14,15). Three different Greek words are involved, yet the meanings are very close: a debt is an obligation; a sin is a missing of the mark; a trespass is a straying from the path—but all are shortcomings in the sight of God for which we need forgiveness. And, significantly, forgiveness is sought in the measure that "we forgive our debtors". Some manuscripts read "*have* forgiven", but in the end the meaning is the same: in coming to God for forgiveness we must have dismissed from our minds any hurt our brother might have caused us.

The confession of sins to be forgiven implies our repentance—without which we cannot expect forgiveness. Also implied is the fact that though, by his death, our Lord atoned for sin, and by belief and baptism we are associated in that perfect work of redemption, nevertheless we still sin and are in constant, daily, need of forgiveness: "If any man sin, we have an advocate with the Father, Jesus Christ the righteous" (1 John 2:1).

"Lead us not into temptation"

God put trials in the way of His children, yet not in the sense of pitfalls to make them sin. More likely, the sense here is, 'Do not allow us to be led into temptation'. We should avoid situations that might try or tempt us; but, knowing how poor we are at keeping clear of evil, we must also seek God's help and blessing. To be safeguarded from our own weaknesses is one of our greatest needs.

In the upper room, the Lord, knowing Simon Peter's vulnerability, said, "Simon, Simon, behold, Satan hath desired to have you, that he may sift you as wheat: but I have prayed for thee, that thy faith fail not" (Luke 22:31,32). In Gethsemane, the Lord exhorted his disciples: "Pray that ye enter not into temptation" (verses 40,46)—and just as Jesus himself had an angel to strengthen him (verse 43), so surely his followers could count on angelic assistance.

69

James writes: "Count it all joy when ye fall into divers temptations" (1:2). Is there a contradiction with the phrase in the Lord's Prayer? There cannot be: James is not encouraging us to desire or seek temptations (or trials); but if we find ourselves in them, to see their positive benefits.

"Deliver us from evil"

Almost identical words occur in the prayer of Jabez:

> "Oh, that thou wouldest bless me indeed, and enlarge my border, and that thine hand might be with me, and that thou wouldest *keep me from evil*, that it be not to my sorrow!" (1 Chronicles 4:10, RV)

Some have seen this curious prayer, almost hidden in a list of names, as a rather selfish prayer, merely seeking prosperity—and it has been seized upon by 'Christian' businessmen as a prayer to be prayed by executives seeking to increase company profits! The prayer of Jabez is no more than any faithful Israelite might pray: that God's gracious hand would be upon him, and protect him from evil.

Jesus sought to be kept from evil. He prayed: "O my Father, if it be possible, let this cup pass from me: nevertheless not as I will, but as thou wilt" (Matthew 26:39). Only one like us, made "a little lower than the angels", would ask if there was another way—and there was none. He acknowledged his total dependence upon God to keep him from trials that he might be unable to bear.

For us, these last two petitions are an acknowledgement that we cannot fend off temptation and evil without the Father's gracious help. Paul acknowledged his need: "The Lord stood with me … and I was delivered out of the mouth of the lion. And the Lord shall *deliver me from every evil work*, and will preserve me unto his heavenly kingdom: to whom be glory for ever and ever" (2 Timothy 4:17,18).

"Thine is the kingdom, the power, and the glory"

The words which conclude the Lord's Prayer in Matthew's Gospel are often referred to as the 'doxology'. (Luke's rendering omits the doxology and finishes with "deliver us from evil".) Although many modern versions omit the doxology, even from Matthew's account, we trust the authenticity of those manuscripts that retain it. Surely it is right that the Prayer concludes with praise—acknowledging God's glory and power. Paul's words to Timothy, mentioned on the previous page, provide additional evidence: although Paul is not quoting the Lord's Prayer word for word, it is very significant that he should refer to being *delivered from evil*, then refer to *the kingdom*, and then add, "to whom be *glory for ever and ever. Amen*" (2 Timothy 4:18).

Some have objected that the Lord's Prayer neglects the giving of thanks to God. Our thanks may not be explicit but gratitude is surely implied by our expressions of dependence upon God, and by the ascriptions of honour and praise, particularly in these closing words.

"Amen"

And so we give assent (see chapter 23—"Amen") to this brief but matchless Prayer. We call it 'The Lord's Prayer'. It is a pattern prayer given by the Lord to the disciples as a basis for their prayers—and ours. But it is in another sense the *Lord's* prayer: it was the essence of his own pilgrimage before God; each phrase reflects what Jesus lived for; his whole life was an embodiment of that prayer. Words from the pen of Brother L. G. Sargent* (whose writing on this subject has been invaluable in the preparation of this chapter) come to mind: 'How often the cross proves the true interpreter of the prayer!'

Every petition had its outworking in Christ's life. God was his Father; in all he did, he hallowed God's name; he is the heir to God's kingdom; he submitted to his Father's will; he was the bread of life; on the cross he sought forgiveness for others, and through his obedience made our forgiveness possible; though made like us, he resisted temptation and was delivered from evil. For him, truly, we give God glory for ever.

---

*Brother L. G. Sargent, *The Teaching of the Master: A Study of the Sermon on the Mount*, pages 166-204.

*Our heavenly Father, hear
The prayer we offer now;
Thy name be hallowed far and near;
To Thee all nations bow.*

*Thy kingdom come: Thy will
On earth be done in love,
As angels quick with love fulfil
Thy perfect law above.*

*Our daily bread supply
While by Thy word we live:
The guilt of our iniquity
Forgive, as we forgive.*

*From dark temptation's power,
From fleshly lusts, defend:
Deliver in the evil hour,
And guide us to the end.*

*Thine, then, for ever be
All glory, power divine;
The sceptre, throne, and majesty
Of heaven and earth are thine.*

HYMN 162

13

THE FIRST CENTURY ECCLESIA

After Jesus' death and resurrection, believers stood in a new relationship with God. Bringing their praise and petitions through the risen Christ, they "continued stedfastly" in prayer, setting a pattern for ecclesial life today.

FROM the outset of his ministry, the Lord Jesus Christ had encouraged his disciples to bring their requests in prayer to God:

"Ask, and it shall be given you; seek, and ye shall find; knock, and it shall be opened unto you ... If ye, being evil, know how to give good gifts unto your children, how much more shall your Father which is in heaven give good things to them that ask him?"   (Matthew 7:7-11)

"Hitherto have ye asked nothing in my name"

The Lord had encouraged them along the path of prayer, and given them a pattern prayer to follow. But so far, it would appear that he had not instructed them to pray through him. As his hour drew near, he began to prepare them for the time when he would not be present; a time, moreover, when they would have the new experience of addressing their prayers to God in his name:

"Hitherto have ye asked nothing in my name: ask, and ye shall receive, that your joy may be full."   (John 16:24)

It is John, particularly, who records how Jesus prepared his followers for a future without him. As early as chapter 7, the Master explains: "I go unto him that sent me" (7:33).

In chapter 13, we read: "Yet a little while I am with you ... Whither I go, ye cannot come" (13:33). The bewildered band cannot take it in, and Thomas protests: "Lord, we know not whither thou goest; and how can we know the way?" (14:5).

It is then, in chapters 14-16, that John records the many assurances Jesus gave the disciples before his arrest and crucifixion, and with these assurances come pointers to the way they are now to approach the Father—through him:

"I am the way, the truth, and the life: no man cometh unto the Father, but *by me*." (14:6)

"Whatsoever ye shall ask *in my name*, that will I do, that the Father may be glorified in the Son. If ye shall ask any thing *in my name*, I will do it." (14:13,14)

"Whatsoever ye shall ask the Father *in my name*, he will give it you." (15:7,16; 16:23)

The Comforter*

The Lord is explaining his role as intercessor between believers and the Father. But he is promising something more than just his intercession in prayer:

"I will pray the Father, and he shall give you another Comforter, that he may abide with you for ever; even the Spirit of truth ... I will not leave you comfortless: I will come to you ... If a man love me, he will keep my words: and my Father will love him, and we will come unto him, and make our abode with him." (14:16-18,23)

This is what the perplexed disciples needed: the assurance that their Lord—and the Father Himself—would continue to be with them. Though he had to die, rise from the dead, and be taken from them, the Lord Jesus Christ would continue to guide and strengthen them in their work for him.

After his resurrection, Jesus told them: "All power is given unto me in heaven and in earth" (Matthew 28:18).

*More detailed expositions of the work of the Comforter will be found in Brother Alfred Nicholls' book, *The Spirit of God*, and Brother Fred Pearce's *God's Spirit in Work and Word*.

The risen Christ would invoke God's power—the power of the Holy Spirit—to assist the infant ecclesia. As God had been Israel's Comforter (see, for example, Isaiah 52:9), so now the exalted Christ would be a Comforter ('counsel', 'advocate', 'one called alongside')—teaching the believers; bringing things to their remembrance; testifying and reproving; guiding them into all truth; showing them things to come; enabling some to speak in tongues and perform miracles (John 14:26; 15:26; 16:7-13; Acts 2:33; Mark 16:20). In the language of Revelation 2:1, he would continue to walk among the lampstands.

The work of the Comforter was concerned especially with the growth of the first century ecclesias. Once they had the inspired writings of the New Testament, the ecclesias were less dependent on the support they had needed in the early days, and the Spirit gifts ceased. Yet the Lord's promise, "Lo, I am with you alway, even unto the end of the world" (Matthew 28:20), would remain true.

A New Relationship

For the apostles who, at Pentecost, went forth in joy and confidence to preach the Gospel, there was an entirely new basis for prayer. The Lamb of God had died, a sacrifice for sin, and God had raised him from the dead. Believers now had a High Priest at God's right hand, the mediator of the new covenant and their intercessor in prayer:

> "For Christ is not entered into the holy places made with hands ... but into heaven itself, now to appear in the presence of God for us."   (Hebrews 9:24)

The Lord Jesus was no longer the mortal Son of man, but the glorified and exalted Son of God. The Lord said to Mary Magdalene: "Go to my brethren, and say unto them, I ascend unto my Father, and your Father; and to my God, and your God" (John 20:17)—words which told them that they could now approach the Father and present their requests in Christ's name.

Mark summarises the new situation in which those first-century believers found themselves:

"So then after the Lord had spoken unto them, he was received up into heaven, and sat on the right hand of God. And they went forth, and preached every where, the Lord working with them, and confirming the word with signs following." (16:19,20)

Although these verses do not speak of prayer as such, they eloquently describe the new relationship between the believer and God as a result of the work of the Saviour. The one whom the disciples had called Master was now exalted as Lord; Jesus of Nazareth was now confirmed to be the Christ. As Peter declared to the Jews in Jerusalem:

"God hath made that same Jesus, whom ye have crucified, both Lord and Christ." (Acts 2:36)

Prayer in Acts

These wonderful truths will, very probably, have sunk in only slowly as the apostles gathered in Jerusalem and began to undertake the commission their Lord had left them. Acts introduces us to a community seized with excitement about the work that lay ahead. They went forth preaching fearlessly and in new-found strength. It is true that for a time they were aided by the gifts of the Spirit, but as we read these chapters we are impressed how restrained they were in the exercise of those gifts, and how greatly dependent they were on prayer.

It is not surprising, of course, that Luke, whose Gospel record was so full of references to prayer, should lay such stress on prayer in his book of Acts as well. Returning to Jerusalem after witnessing the ascension of their Lord, the first activity in which the eleven engaged was prayer:

"These all continued with one accord in prayer and supplication, with the women, and Mary the mother of Jesus, and with his brethren." (1:14)

Before appointing a successor to Judas Iscariot,

"They prayed, and said, Thou, Lord, which knowest the hearts of all men, show whether of these two thou hast chosen." (1:24)

Doctrine, Fellowship, Breaking of Bread, Prayers

The spectacular success of the preaching did not deflect the young ecclesia from acts of fellowship and devotion, and we begin to see the newly formed body of Christ at prayer:

> "They continued stedfastly in the apostles' doctrine and fellowship, and in breaking of bread, *and in prayers ... praising God*, and having favour with all the people."
> (2:42-47)

When they were threatened by the rulers, they lifted up their voices with one accord. Their petition was not for their own safety or comfort, but that they might be allowed to continue their witness:

> "Now, Lord, behold their threatenings: and grant unto thy servants, that with all boldness they may speak thy word ... and that signs and wonders may be done by the name of thy holy child Jesus."
> (4:24-30)

As far as the rest of Acts is concerned, we can do little more than note, very briefly, the main references to prayer. In chapter 6, we read of the appointment of "seven men of honest report" who were to take charge of pastoral ministrations in the growing community, enabling the Twelve to give themselves "continually to prayer, and to the ministry of the word" (6:3,4). The apostles prayed and laid hands on those setting out on a mission (6:6; 13:3; 14:23). Stephen died, "calling upon God" (7:59,60). Paul was praying when Ananias found him (9:11; cf. 22:17). Peter was praying when he received the vision of the sheet let down from heaven (10:9); and when Peter was in prison, the ecclesia prayed earnestly on his behalf (12:5,12). When establishing ecclesias and ordaining elders, the apostles "prayed with fasting" (14:23). In the prison at Philippi, Paul and Silas prayed and sang praises (16:25); and Paul, calling the elders of Ephesus to Miletus, "kneeled down and prayed with them all" (20:36; cf. 21:5).

Prayer in Ecclesial Life Today

From these examples of the first century ecclesia at prayer we can learn much that is relevant and vital for ecclesial life today. Prayer was foremost in their corporate (and no doubt also their personal) lives. Prayer preceded their decisions; when faced with difficulties they resorted straight away to prayer.

For us, in this far-off 21st century, ecclesial life is still based on the principles epitomised in Acts 2:42—(1) the apostles' doctrine; (2) fellowship; (3) the breaking of bread; and (4) prayers. Incidentally, "doctrine" in this context carries as much the meaning of "teaching" or "preaching" as of a system of beliefs to be observed: in other words (as we have just seen in the quotation from Acts 4) the ecclesia's witness was paramount. It would not be too wide of the mark to re-word those four facets of ecclesial life as (1) preaching the true Gospel; (2) strengthening the fellowship of the ecclesia; (3) meeting regularly for breaking of bread; (4) coming together "with one accord" for prayer.

The position of prayer in fourth place does not mean that prayer is of least importance; it is just as important as those other aspects of ecclesial life, and essential to each of them. So do *we* "continue stedfastly … in prayers"? Is there in *our* meetings an atmosphere of reverent devotion and worship; of joyful praise and thankfulness? Is there opportunity for fervent supplication on behalf of persons who are in difficulty or causes that are in need?

Prayer Meetings

For some, the reaction to such questions may be to suggest the holding of special prayer meetings—and in certain circumstances these are right. If the background to a difficult situation or a grievous problem requires explanation, and prayers of extra intensity are called for, then a separate meeting may be advisable. Otherwise, there is no reason why our memorial service, or for that matter the Bible Class, should not provide the occasion to bring our concerns to God.

14

PRAYER IN THE EPISTLES

The apostles were men of prayer, and in their letters we find examples of their own prayers for the ecclesias and exhortations to be constant in prayer. Paul in particular can teach us much about prayer in ecclesial life today.

AMONG Bible examples of men of prayer, Paul must surely rank as one of the greatest—after the Lord Jesus Christ. It is not just that the Acts of the Apostles record him as being regularly at prayer (9:11; 16:25; 20:36; 21:5; 28:8); in his epistles too we find constant evidence of Paul's dependence on prayer, while the language of his letters is often the language of prayer.

Letters Full of Prayer

Throughout the epistles there are countless phrases which, although not prayers as we normally think of them, express the desires of the apostle which only God can fulfil. Thus the greeting at the start of so many of the letters, "Grace to you and peace from God our Father, and the Lord Jesus Christ" (Romans 1:7 etc.), is actually a prayer—it is Paul's petition that God and the Lord Jesus Christ would grant to the Romans grace and peace. And the writer's prayers continue: "I thank my God through Jesus Christ for you all ... without ceasing I make mention of you always in my prayers" (1:8,9). Romans contains many more instances; one of the loveliest is in chapter 15:

"Now the God of patience and consolation grant you to be likeminded one toward another according to Christ

Jesus: that ye may with one mind and one mouth glorify God, even the Father of our Lord Jesus Christ ... The God of hope fill you with all joy and peace in believing, that ye may abound in hope ... The God of peace be with you all. Amen." (Romans 15:5,6,13,33)

What depths of spiritual meaning there are in these few verses: Paul wants the believers in Rome to be like-minded, applying Godly patience in their ecclesial affairs; for then, if they are of one mind, they can properly glorify God; and, if they truly believe, God will grant them joy, peace and hope. Do we pray like this? Brethren do pray for help in achieving greater unity and harmony in our fellowship together, though not always in such specific terms. How often does a president ask God to grant us joy and peace in believing? And do we fill *our* letters (telephone calls, e-mails) with petitions to the Father as Paul does here?

Wonder at the Work of God

In his letter to the Ephesians, Paul switches seamlessly between exposition, worship and prayer. It is as if his mind cannot dwell on the magnificence of the Gospel message without bursting forth in praise and wonder—and prayer—at the work of God and the obedience of His Son:

"Blessed be the God and Father of our Lord Jesus Christ, who hath blessed us with all spiritual blessings in heavenly places in Christ: according as he hath chosen us in him before the foundation of the world ... Wherefore I ... cease not to give thanks for you, making mention of you in my prayers; that the God of our Lord Jesus Christ, the Father of glory, may give unto you the spirit of wisdom and revelation in the knowledge of him ..."
(Ephesians 1:3,4,15-17)

"I bow my knees unto the Father"

The spirit of prayer continues in chapter 3, where the apostle first reflects on his own position in relation to the Gospel, contemplating the amazing privilege which was his in being commissioned to "preach among the Gentiles the unsearchable riches of Christ; and to make all men see what is the fellowship of the mystery" (verses 8,9). He ponders the marvellous truth that we can "have boldness and access in confidence through our faith in him" (verse 12, RV). In the first two chapters, he has already lifted his readers into "heavenly places", and now having come, as it were, into the very presence of God, and having "boldness and access in confidence" through Christ Jesus, he prays with unsurpassed eloquence—

"For this cause I bow my knees unto the Father of our Lord Jesus Christ ... that he would grant you, according to the riches of his glory, to be strengthened with might by his Spirit in the inner man; that Christ may dwell in your hearts by faith; that ye, being rooted and grounded in love, may be able to comprehend with all saints what is the breadth, and length, and depth, and height; and to know the love of Christ, which passeth knowledge, that ye might be filled with all the fulness of God. Now unto him that is able to do exceeding abundantly above all that we ask or think, according to the power that worketh in us, unto him be glory ... Amen." (3:14-21)

Paul's desires for those he loved

Overflowing in praise to God, Paul pours out his desires for those he loved. Foremost among those desires is that they, "being rooted and grounded in love" might "know the love of Christ" and "be filled with all the fulness of God". This is no mere show of fine-sounding phrases (of which we can sometimes be guilty in our prayers) but an expression of what God will grant to those who sincerely seek to know Him and His Son. Paul had himself been "strengthened with might by his Spirit in the inner man" (verse 16); Christ dwelt in Paul's own heart (verse 17); Paul himself comprehended, with all saints, the love of Christ (verses 18,19); and he knew from experience that God was "able to do exceeding abundantly above all that we ask or think". Confident in that experience, the apostle could pray for the same blessings to be granted to his readers.

So do our prayers match those of Paul? Should they? There is surely nothing in the language of Pauline prayers that could be uttered only by the Spirit-guided apostles of the first century: we may not have their experience and authority but, just as they followed the instruction of their Lord as far as prayer was concerned, so can we—drawing on the examples of Christ and his apostles, as well as the men and women of prayer in earlier times.

And this is where, if we are heedless of those examples, we run into danger. Diminishing respect for and understanding of the Word of God today has led to innovations in prayer in the churches of Christendom which are not in accordance with sound doctrine: prayers to the Holy Spirit, prayers solely to Jesus without reference to God, prayers to Mary, prayers to 'saints'; dependence on set prayers from prayer books; congregational prayers led by female clergy—indeed the very idea that a priesthood is needed for the offering of acceptable prayer to God. Our prayers are to be patterned on Biblical examples, of which we have so many—in both Old and New Testaments.

Intensity and Perseverance

With the example of Paul before us, how can we possibly imagine that casual and perfunctory prayers are all that God requires of us? Paul's prayers were intense: in spite of all the distractions and demands around him—indeed because of them—he prayed "with all perseverance" (Ephesians 6:18). "Without ceasing I have remembrance of thee in my prayers night and day" (2 Timothy 1:3; cf. Colossians 1:3,9; 1 Thessalonians 1:2,3; 2:13; 3:10; 5:17; 2 Thessalonians 1:11; Philemon 4).

Three times Paul besought the Lord concerning his "thorn in the flesh" (2 Corinthians 12:7-9). Can this be so? Would he not have prayed times without number? Perhaps he was acting on the Lord's words, that "this kind goeth not out but by prayer and fasting" (Matthew 17:21), so that on three particular occasions, with prayer and fasting, he may have made a very special effort to beseech God. Whatever Paul did, we have to learn to pray, not with drama and ostentation, but with quiet persistence and in complete faith that whatever the outcome, it is God's will.

Praying "in a tongue"

There are references in 1 Corinthians 14 to praying and the giving of thanks "in a tongue": this was an experience limited to those who had the gift of tongues in the apostolic age—and from Paul's language it is clear that the gift was being misused: "How can anyone in the position of an outsider say 'Amen' to your thanksgiving when he does not know what you are saying?" (verse 16, ESV). It seems that Spirit gifts were often a hindrance rather than a help in ecclesial prayers. Today, there is no danger from the misapplication of gifts of tongues, though there is still a risk of prayers being incomprehensible if brethren are 'carried away' in language which others find difficult to follow.

"Pray for us"

Sometimes it may seem that those who minister to the ecclesia's and the Brotherhood's needs are supremely strong and self-sufficient—eloquent in their prayers on behalf of others, and in no particular need themselves. Paul was certainly not like this, and the true leaders and elders amongst us are similarly always in need of God's help and of the prayers of others.

"Brethren, pray for us." (1 Thessalonians 5:25)

"Finally, brethren, pray for us, that the word of the Lord may have free course, and be glorified ..."
(2 Thessalonians 3:1; cf. Hebrews 13:18)

Other New Testament Prayers

While we have concentrated on the prayers of Paul, the epistles of James, Peter, John and Jude follow similar patterns, proving a consistency of New Testament practice which we should imitate. It is interesting that when John addresses the seven ecclesias in the book of Revelation, he adopts the prayer-like greeting which we find at the commencement of so many of Paul's and Peter's letters:

"John to the seven churches which are in Asia: Grace be unto you, and peace ... " (Revelation 1:4)

But we conclude this chapter with that masterpiece of compact and perfect prayer in Jude's epistle:

> *Now unto him that is able to keep you from falling, and to present you faultless before the presence of his glory with exceeding joy, to the only wise God our Saviour, be glory and majesty, dominion and power, both now and ever. Amen.*
>
> *(Jude 24,25)*

15

"HE EVER LIVETH TO MAKE INTERCESSION"

By his death the Lord Jesus opened a new and living way of access to God: he is the mediator of the new covenant and our intercessor with God in prayer. He is our high priest, our advocate at God's right hand, to plead our cause.

AT the end of our prayers (or sometimes at the start) we use one of a small number of phrases to acknowledge the intercession of Christ by which we are privileged to address God—for example, "through Jesus Christ our Lord", "for Jesus' sake", or "in Christ's name". Whichever phrase we employ, we are claiming access to that "new and living way" (Hebrews 10:20) which the sacrifice of Christ has opened to us.

"Through our Lord Jesus Christ"

Must we always use such a phrase? Which form is best? Phrases including "through" possibly have the greatest scriptural support, as the following examples show:

"I thank my God *through Jesus Christ* for you all ... To God only wise, be glory *through Jesus Christ* for ever."
(Romans 1:8; 16:27)

"*Through him* (AV, by him) then let us continually offer up a sacrifice of praise to God, that is, the fruit of lips that acknowledge his name." (Hebrews 13:15, ESV)

"You yourselves like living stones are being built up as a spiritual house, to be a holy priesthood, to offer spiritual sacrifices acceptable to God *through* (AV, by) *Jesus Christ*."   (1 Peter 2:5, ESV)

"In Christ's name", however, also has scripture precedent, particularly from John's Gospel:

"Whatsoever ye shall ask the Father *in my name*, he will give it you ..."   (John 16:23 etc.)

"(Give) thanks always for all things unto God and the Father *in the name of our Lord Jesus Christ*."
                              (Ephesians 5:20; Colossians 3:17)

"For Jesus' sake"

"For Jesus' sake" is also scripturally based, though it is harder to find the phrase actually used in an example of prayer in the New Testament. Of course, there are numerous passages that speak of witnessing, suffering, or being hated "for Jesus' sake" (e.g. Matthew 10:22; Acts 9:16; Revelation 2:3). Similar phrases are used, moreover, in connection with our Lord's work of redemption—"your sins are forgiven you for his name's sake" (1 John 2:12).

In New Testament Greek, the phrase translated into English as "for ... sake" is simply a preposition meaning 'through', 'because of', 'on behalf of', or 'on account of'. When we ask God to hear our prayer "for Jesus' sake", we are asking Him to hear us *through* Jesus, *because of* or *on account of* what our Lord achieved on our behalf by laying down his life.

Occasionally, a brother may use other phrases: "by the merits of our Saviour Jesus Christ", or "through our high priest at thy right hand"—again, acknowledging that the privilege of prayer is ours as a result of Christ's sacrifice.

Is a prayer invalidated before God if we omit to include one of the above phrases? There are certainly prayers recorded in the New Testament without such a phrase. The point is surely that, whether or not we say "through Jesus Christ", we recognise by other words, or at least in unspoken thought, that our petitions are heard only by virtue of our high priest and mediator at God's right hand.

Mediatorship

We have touched on mediatorship before, particularly in its Old Testament context; now we shall look at the role of the Lord Jesus Christ as our mediator with God. The word translated "mediator" occurs six times in the New Testament; it is also to be found in the Septuagint (i.e. Greek) version of Job, a passage which very usefully defines its original meaning:

> "For he is not a man, as I am, that I should answer him, and we should come together in judgment. Neither is there any *daysman* betwixt us, that might lay his hand upon us both."   (Job 9:32,33)

Job looked in vain for a "daysman" or go-between; his situation was that of all mankind after the Fall—a position of estrangement from God. Before Christ, man could come to God through angels, priests and prophets, and particularly by virtue of the rituals of the Law of Moses. These, however, were shadows of what was to come: in the Lord Jesus Christ God provided the perfect mediator:

> "He is the mediator of a better covenant, which was established upon better promises."
>   (Hebrews 8:6; see also 9:15; 12:24)

The mediator of the old covenant at Sinai was Moses (Exodus 24:8; cf. Galatians 3:19,20). And just as that was ratified by the shedding of blood, so too was the new covenant in Christ: "Now in Christ Jesus ye who sometimes were far off are made nigh by the blood of Christ" (Ephesians 2:13; cf. 1 Peter 3:18).

Besides the references to "mediator" in Galatians and Hebrews, there is one other in 1 Timothy:

> "For there is one God, and one mediator between God and men, the man Christ Jesus; who gave himself a ransom for all."   (1 Timothy 2:5,6)

The context here is clearly that of prayer. Verse 1 of the chapter introduces the subject of prayer: "I exhort therefore, that, first of all, supplications, prayers, intercessions, and giving of thanks, be made for all men" and verse 8 continues: "I will therefore that men pray every where, lifting up holy hands". Verse 5 summarises in majestic brevity the means whereby such prayer is possible—through Christ, the one mediator between God and men.

Christ our Intercessor

Though "mediator" is used in 1 Timothy 2:5 in connection with prayer, elsewhere the more commonly used word is "intercessor". In the New Testament, there are three original Greek words, and they all convey the idea of 'meeting' or 'conversation'. By Christ's sacrifice, a meeting between man and God—in other words, prayer—has been made possible; our high priest intercedes for us:

> "Wherefore he is able also to save them to the uttermost that come unto God by him, seeing he ever liveth to make intercession for them." (Hebrews 7:25)

> "Having therefore, brethren, boldness to enter into the holiest by the blood of Jesus, by a new and living way … and having an high priest over the house of God; let us draw near with a true heart in full assurance of faith …" (10:19-22)

How does the Lord intercede?

But how does he intercede for us? There is a danger that we view the work of Christ in heaven as something akin to that of a telephone switchboard operator—mechanically passing on messages to God. This is far from the truth, for the one at God's right hand is a living Lord, vitally concerned about our needs and our wish to pray through him.

Paul helps us to understand the process of intercession in Romans:

> "Likewise the Spirit also helpeth our infirmities: for we know not what we should pray for as we ought: but the Spirit itself maketh intercession for us with groanings which cannot be uttered. And he that searcheth the hearts knoweth what is the mind of the Spirit, because

he maketh intercession for the saints according to the will of God." (8:26,27)

This passage presents a challenge: if the Lord Jesus Christ is our intercessor, why does Paul say, "the Spirit itself maketh intercession"?

There are those in the churches who believe that the Holy Spirit, a person of the Trinity, intercedes in prayer: this cannot be the meaning. By his use of the word "Spirit", does Paul simply mean Christ? This is a more acceptable interpretation, particularly as Christ is the subject of a very similar statement later on in the same chapter:

"It is Christ that died, yea rather, that is risen again, who is even at the right hand of God, *who also maketh intercession for us.*" (verse 34)

The suggestion is, then, that in verses 26 and 27, too, Paul has Christ in mind, but chooses to refer to him as one who is "spirit"—the whole of Romans 8 is, after all, about those who are "in the spirit".

But this leads on to another, and quite compelling, way of looking at this passage. From verse 1 onwards, Paul is building up the idea that those who are "in Christ Jesus" walk "after the spirit"; they are "spiritually minded" (verse 6); in them dwells "the spirit of God" and "the spirit of Christ" (verses 9-11).* Paul expresses the same truth elsewhere in the words, "We have the *mind* of Christ" (1 Corinthians 2:16).

So what Paul seems to be saying is that those with the mind of Christ have infirmities; they do not know how to pray; but God ("he that searcheth the hearts") knows what is in their mind—and a 'meeting of minds' takes place (another way of describing intercession). And this in no way contradicts verse 34, which confirms that it is, in the end, "Christ Jesus ... who is at the right hand of God, who indeed is interceding for us" (ESV).

---

*"Spirit" may be printed with a capital or small 's', and this can be misleading: there is no distinction between capital and small letters in the original.

The following verses from Ephesians may serve to underline what we have concluded so far:

"For *through him* we both have access *in one Spirit* to the Father ... In Christ Jesus our Lord ... we have boldness and access with confidence through our faith in him." (Ephesians 2:18; 3:11,12, ESV)

"Groanings which cannot be uttered"

One of the other difficulties in Romans 8 is the reference to "groanings". Verses 22,23 refer to the fact that "the whole creation groaneth ... we ourselves groan within ourselves". A related word is then used in the context of intercession: "The Spirit itself maketh intercession [for us] with groanings which cannot be uttered" (verse 26).

It would seem that, as in verse 23, it is "we ourselves" who groan—we struggle to find words to express our needs to God. On the other hand, some would argue that the groanings refer to the pleadings of the Lord himself, as he explains to the Father our needs and longings in words which we can never know or comprehend.

From God through Christ—to Us

There is a tendency to concentrate so much on Christ's intercession as our high priest God-ward, that we may fail to acknowledge what he does in mediating grace and kindness *from God toward us*. We should never cease to marvel at the promise of God to watch over us, to answer prayer, to supply our needs, and to show us the way of truth in Christ:

"He who did not spare his own Son but gave him up for us all, how *will he not also with him* graciously give us all things? ... (Nothing) will be able to separate us from *the love of God in Christ Jesus our Lord*." (Romans 8:32,39, ESV)

"The peace of God, which passeth all understanding, shall keep your hearts and minds *through Christ Jesus* ... *My God* shall supply all your need according to his riches in glory *by Christ Jesus*." (Philippians 4:7,19)

"Now *our Lord Jesus Christ himself, and God, even our Father,* which hath loved us, and hath given us everlasting consolation and good hope through grace, comfort your hearts, and stablish you in every good word and work." (2 Thessalonians 2:16,17)

"Now *the God of peace*, that brought again from the dead our Lord Jesus, that great shepherd of the sheep, through the blood of the everlasting covenant, make you perfect in every good work to do his will, *working in you* that which is well-pleasing in his sight, *through Jesus Christ.*" (Hebrews 13:20,21)

"Who is sufficient for these things?"

We stand back in wonder at the many facets of the character and work of our Lord Jesus Christ—all that he was, and all that he accomplished on our behalf. He is the unique daysman that Job never knew and for which he yearned; he is the mediator of the new covenant; he is the high priest who has entered the holiest once for all, with his own blood, to atone for his people; he is the advocate with the Father, one 'called alongside', who pleads for his disciples; he is our faithful intercessor at God's right hand. And he is the one who ministers to our needs, dispensing the rich blessings his Father is pleased to shower on those who truly seek Him.

Though we are not worthy of these things, we grasp with thankfulness the way of salvation and hope of life which our Redeemer has opened for us, and show our gratitude in loving service.

O God in highest heaven,
  Our God that hearest prayer,
Through Christ — whom Thou hast given,
  Our Advocate, Thine Heir;
Now, strong in hope, united,
  Around Thy feast we meet;
Receive from him our incense;
  He is Thy Mercy-seat …

Now through Thy greater Prophet,
  Seated at Thy right hand,
May prayer be like a rampart
  As 'gainst the foe we stand.
For Abraham's God is our God,
  And Isaac's God is ours;
Ours is the God of Jacob
  With His almighty powers.

HYMN 238, VERSES 1 & 3

16

"THAT ALL MEN SHOULD HONOUR THE SON"

Prayer is addressed to God, and all praise and worship is ultimately to His glory. It is right, however, to give honour to the Lord Jesus Christ; and we can properly offer love and devotion to him, to whom "every knee shall bow".

THE Lord Jesus Christ has many titles and roles. He is the Son of God, the Son of Man, the Lamb of God, the Redeemer of mankind, the Mediator of the new covenant. He is our Saviour, our Master, our High Priest, our Intercessor at God's right hand, and our coming King. In a more personal way, he is—or should be—our companion on the path to the kingdom, one who knows our needs, who himself experienced our trials. He is the Lord we love, and in whom we confide.

We have a living relationship with the Lord Jesus Christ. Through him we address our prayers to the Father; whilst he also mediates, from God to us, the love and peace of God, "working in you that which is well-pleasing in his sight, through Jesus Christ" (Hebrews 13:21).

A Living Relationship

We cannot claim to have a living relationship with the Son of God if we do not acknowledge his continuing and constant activity in heaven on our behalf. As was emphasised in the previous chapter, a phrase such as "through Jesus Christ our Lord" is not just a formula by which prayer finds its way to God: in acknowledging Christ's gracious work in intercession, we acknowledge his abiding presence in our lives and our dependence on him in our walk as disciples.

Sometimes—happily, not often—a prayer may be offered which addresses God and scarcely mentions His Son. It goes without saying, of course, that God is supreme: to Him all glory is ultimately due; but our religion is incomplete and our faith is barren if our walk with God does not involve the Lord Jesus Christ and give him honour.

During his ministry on earth, the disciples worshipped him (Matthew 14:33; 28:9,17). They did not honour him *instead of* God: it is noteworthy, for example, that as Jesus ascended to heaven:

> "They *worshipped him*, and returned to Jerusalem with great joy: and were continually in the temple, *praising and blessing God.*" (Luke 24:52,53)

The risen Christ was honoured, and God was praised.

Apostolic Prayers

What do the scriptures tell us about the relationship between believers and Christ *after* his ascension? It is significant that the disciples were referred to as those who "called on his name" (Acts 2:21; 9:14,21; 22:16; 1 Corinthians 1:2; 2 Timothy 2:22). The apostles prayed for guidance when choosing a successor to Judas: "Thou, Lord, which knowest the hearts of all men, shew whether of these two thou hast chosen" (Acts 1:24)—and bearing in mind that it was Jesus who chose the original Twelve, it is reasonable to say that the "Lord" here is Jesus and not God.

Stephen saw Christ standing on the right hand of God and "as they were stoning Stephen, he called out, 'Lord Jesus, receive my spirit'" (Acts 7:59, ESV). Saul of Tarsus spoke to Jesus, who was revealed to him in blinding light on the Damascus road and subsequently in a trance (9:3-7; 22:6-10,17-21). Ananias, too, conversed with Jesus (9:10-17). Later, Paul had further reassurances in vision from his Lord (18:9,10; 23:11).

All of these occurrences have one thing in common. They are responses to specific appearances of the Lord Jesus. He had met with them and spoken with them after his resurrection. After his ascension, he had appeared to Stephen. On the Damascus road, he had spoken to Saul. He had appeared in a vision to Ananias, giving him instructions concerning Saul. And the apostle John had received directly from Jesus' angel those visions of events that would affect the future of the ecclesia of Christ (Revelation 1:1). The prayers we have reviewed are the natural responses of those *to whom the Lord appeared.*

And the apostles continue to take it for granted that they can speak to the Lord: they know that the Lord is alive and working with them as they bear witness to his name. Paul writes to Timothy: "I thank Christ Jesus our Lord, who hath enabled me ..." (1 Timothy 1:12); and it is again Paul who "besought the Lord thrice" about his affliction—and received the Lord's response (2 Corinthians 12:8,9). The scriptures close, moreover, with a prayer from John: "Even so, come, Lord Jesus" (Revelation 22:20).

"Worship God"

Nevertheless, the overwhelming evidence of the New Testament, including the pattern set by Jesus himself in the Lord's Prayer, is that praise, petition and thanks should be addressed to the Father: the young ecclesias in fact were exhorted to address their prayers to God— through the Lord Jesus Christ:

"In every thing by prayer and supplication with thanksgiving let your requests be made known unto God."   (Philippians 4:6)

"Whatsoever ye do in word or deed, do all in the name of the Lord Jesus, giving thanks to God and the Father by him."   (Colossians 3:17)

There is also the indirect evidence of John who, when he fell down to worship before the feet of the angel, was told:

"See thou do it not ... worship God."
(Revelation 19:10; 22:8,9)

95

We pray to God, yet we desire to give due honour to the Lord Jesus Christ: how do we maintain the proper balance? Let us look at a few more relevant passages.

"That all men should honour the Son"

Jesus rightly claims the honour due to one who overcame and is exalted to the Father's presence; and he will be honoured and worshipped when he returns in glory to set up his kingdom:

> "The Father … hath committed all judgment unto the Son: that all men should honour the Son, even as they honour the Father. He that honoureth not the Son honoureth not the Father which hath sent him."
> (John 5:22,23)

> "God also hath highly exalted him, and given him a name which is above every name: that at the name of Jesus every knee should bow … and that every tongue should confess that Jesus Christ is Lord, to the glory of God the Father." (Philippians 2:9-11)

> "We see Jesus, who was made a little lower than the angels for the suffering of death, crowned with glory and honour." (Hebrews 2:9)

> "He received from God the Father honour and glory, when there came such a voice to him from the excellent glory, This is my beloved Son, in whom I am well pleased." (2 Peter 1:17)

> "Worthy is the Lamb that was slain to receive power, and riches, and wisdom, and strength, and honour, and glory, and blessing." (Revelation 5:12)

Jesus Christ is truly "Lord", to be held in honour by his disciples. If he appeared before us today (and one day, in God's pleasure, he will), our instinctive reaction would be to bow in spontaneous adoration: we could not help ourselves. We may just hesitate to admit that this would be our reaction, and the reason is understandable—we have never had the experience of meeting our Lord face to face.

In that great day, however, we shall have the opportunity to pour out before him our love and thankfulness.

But while we wait for him to return as King, even in this time of probation, it is appropriate to give honour to Jesus. How shall we do this? Turning to John's gospel we discover the marvellous truth that those who respond to his call, by their very discipleship magnify and glorify their Lord:

> "And all mine are thine, and thine are mine; and *I am glorified in them*." (John 17:10)

"I am glorified in them"

Those who follow Christ not only glorify him by becoming disciples; they also honour him actively by their lives and in their devotions. In 2 Thessalonians 1, Paul describes the day when the Lord Jesus Christ will be revealed from heaven, "when he shall come to be glorified in his saints, and to be admired in all them that believe"; but a few verses later the apostle expresses the hope that *now*, even before that day, "the name of our Lord Jesus Christ *may be glorified in you,* and ye in him" (verses 10,12).

But can we be a little more specific in describing *how* we should honour our Master? We do this by a life devoted to his will, following his example in deeds of kindness, witnessing to his work of redemption, and proclaiming his coming. Yet there is more: the thoughtful disciple will seek moments of quiet devotion in the presence of his Lord; he (and she) will want to find opportunity for communication with the Lord. Some would say this is simply meditation, contemplating and reflecting on the amazing work of Christ for us; others would go so far as to call it conversation—confiding in the risen Master.

Living in Fellowship with Christ

A devout sister once related how she held 'conversations' with her Lord, as with an elder brother: they were not prayers in the usual sense, yet such communion with Christ is possible; it is part of the privilege we have of sharing fellowship with him, and with God through him:

"… as thou, Father, art in me, and I in thee, that they also may be one in us."　　　　　　　　　(John 17:21)

"God is faithful, through whom ye were called into the fellowship of his Son Jesus Christ our Lord."
　　　　　　　　　　　　　　(1 Corinthians 1:9, RV)

"Truly our fellowship is with the Father, and with his Son Jesus Christ."　　　　　　　　　(1 John 1:3)

This fellowship is the privilege of those who are "in Christ". Our position is beautifully described by Paul in Ephesians:

"God … quickened us together with Christ … raised us up with him, and made us to sit with him in the heavenly places, in Christ Jesus … Speaking truth in love, (we) may grow up in all things into him, which is the head, even Christ … We are members of his body."
　　　　　　　　　　(Ephesians 2:4-6; 4:15; 5:30, RV)

As members of Christ's body, therefore, we may surely speak to our head—expressing our love, giving him thanks (as Paul did in 1 Timothy 1:12, already quoted), confessing our weakness and waywardness, and offering humble service by which he is glorified. Then, when we lift our petitions to God in Jesus' name, we shall have confidence that he will know our hearts and intercede.

At first we may not really know what to think or say as we try to focus our minds on our Saviour. It should not be difficult, however, simply to contemplate in silence what he did in obedience to his Father and out of love for his brothers and sisters; then to go a little further and exalt him in our thoughts, resolving to be more like him.

Addressing Christ in our Hymns

And this is surely what we do as we sing many of our hymns. What are sometimes (and rather misleadingly) referred to as 'Hymns to Jesus' are not so much prayers to Jesus, but ascriptions of honour, and reflections on his wonderful life and his work of redemption. Other hymns are in the category of personal devotion and commitment—

which it is perfectly in order for a disciple to make. Others are petitions which he may present to his Father on our behalf. Here are a few examples from the Christadelphian Hymn Book:

> Jesus! Thou Sun of Righteousness,
>   Shed forth thy living rays;
> Stir up thy strength, thy mightiness,
>   And manifest thy praise.
>
> (Hymn 366, verse 1—Bro. David Brown)

> Was there no way for any man to live
>   But thou must die, no joy but through thy grief?
> Is sin so dark that God cannot forgive
>   Save through thy sacrifice, and our belief?
>
> (Hymn 221, verse 2—Bro. L. G. Sargent)

> Lord Jesus, I have promised
>   To serve thee to the end;
> Be thou for ever near me,
>   My Master and my Friend:
> I shall not fear the battle
>   If thou art by my side,
> Nor wander from the pathway,
>   If thou wilt be my guide.
>
> (Hymn 209, verse 1—J. E. Bode)

> Lord, come then in thy Kingdom,
>   Set up on earth thy throne;
> And, lest thy sheep grow weary,
>   Come take them for thine own:
> Now, when the night seems darkest,
>   Come in thy glory bright;
> Come to redeem thine Israel,
>   And turn our faith to sight.
>
> (Hymn 284, verse 3—Bro. E. H. Tipping)

We have suggested that hymns with Christ in view may be seen as *personal* devotions and ascriptions of honour, yet there is something about communal song which is different from mere personal meditation (excellent though that is). Singing allows for *united* dedication, reflection and commitment; singing is an act of fellowship; singing is a discipline that brings together weak and strong—strengthening those who may not be able, on their own, to meditate effectively on their Lord.

A Closer Relationship with Christ

These things will arouse feelings of great inadequacy in most of us—for none can live up to the demands of true fellowship in Christ. Achieving a closer walk with the Lord Jesus Christ comes more easily to one disciple than it does to another, and only over many years do we form that relationship with Christ for which we strive. If we achieve it, however, it will bring us in wonder within God's sanctuary, and into the presence of the Son, to whom "all power is given ... in heaven and in earth" (Matthew 28:18).

The New Testament Doxologies

A 'doxology' is an 'expression of glory' (from the Greek *doxa*, meaning 'glory') and describes phrases such as "To him be glory both now and for ever", which occur in a number of the epistles and Revelation. Often, the glory is ascribed to God Himself: Romans 11:36; 16:27; Galatians 1:5; Ephesians 3:21; Philippians 4:20; 1 Timothy 1:17; 6:16; Hebrews 13:21; 1 Peter 4:11; 5:11; Jude 25; Revelation 7:12. In several passages, however, the glory is ascribed to the Lord Jesus Christ: 2 Timothy 4:18; 2 Peter 3:18 and Revelation 1:6; 5:12,13. Nearly all the doxologies close with "Amen". Here is one example in full:

"But grow in grace, and in the knowledge of our Lord and Saviour Jesus Christ. To him be glory both now and for ever. Amen."　　(2 Peter 3:18)

17

WHAT SHOULD WE PRAY FOR?

We struggle to know what to say, but the example of Godly men and women and the pattern of the Lord's Prayer teach us to bring all our petitions in faith to God. "He is able to do exceeding abundantly above all that we ask or think."

D O we really not know what to pray for? To judge from the prayers spoken at our meetings, and from what we know of the private petitions of those close to us, most disciples have plenty to pray about: they present to the Father their praises and worship; and they have a list of requests, some of which may be intense and urgent—for health, for guidance in life's difficult decisions, for the removal of sorrow, for comfort and strength. Surely, most of us know precisely what we desire of the Lord God.

Expressing our Thoughts before God

There is a phrase in Romans—in a passage we have already looked at in connection with our Lord's work of intercession—which must strike a chord in every disciple's heart: "We know not what we should pray for as we ought" (8:26). What does Paul mean? The point he is expounding here is not that we have no idea what to pray for; rather, that we are poor at expressing ourselves in prayer to God. We struggle to present our desires to the Father, and yet, though we cannot always put our pleadings into suitable words, through our intercessor He hears us: that is the wonder of communication with the Almighty, and that is one of the great privileges of prayer.

Legitimate Petitions

But still we find ourselves asking, What, specifically, should we pray for? We can do no better than model our prayers on the pattern provided by the Lord's Prayer, not necessarily using its exact wording but following its order of priorities and applying them to ourselves:

- Acknowledge our dependence on our Father in heaven.

- Praise God, hallow His Name, and resolve by our actions to glorify God and His Son.

- Thank Him for the message of the Gospel; put the kingdom first and pray earnestly for its coming.

- Seek God's will to be done in our own lives and in the fulfilment of His plan with the world.

- Do not take our material blessings for granted; ask God to provide sufficient for the day.

- Thank God for His Son, and for his death on our behalf; confess our sins, and seek the Father's help in overcoming our weaknesses; forgive those who have offended us; then beseech the Father's forgiveness for Jesus' sake.

- Pray that God will guide us through trials, help us to resist temptation, and to be protected from evil.

- Conclude by acknowledging that all is in God's hand, and give Him glory through the Lord Jesus Christ.

Where we rightly hesitate in our prayers is where it comes to our personal, and possibly selfish, petitions. As always, let Scripture teach us. The examples of men and women of prayer are there for our instruction; let us learn from their experience.

We cannot force God's Hand

Both Abraham and Sarah had longed for a son, but they were slow to accept God's assurance that the promised seed would come; each in turn laughed at the idea of a child being born to parents who were so old. Abraham compounded his doubt by pleading, "O that Ishmael might live before thee!" (Genesis 17:18). The lesson is clear: Abraham and Sarah were certainly not wrong to pray for a child, but they had to learn to "ask in faith, nothing wavering" (James 1:6): by putting forward Ishmael, Abraham was attempting to bring about the fulfilment of God's promise in his own way.

And which of us has not acted similarly? We have asked for some blessing, but then, by our independent actions, we have tried to force God's hand! In the end, with contrition and with overwhelming gratitude, we come to acknowledge that His way—sometimes a quite different answer from the one we had sought—was best.

Examples of men and women of prayer can be multiplied: Moses, Samuel, Hannah, David, Elijah, Hezekiah, Daniel, Ezra, Nehemiah, Mary, Simeon, Anna, Paul—and others. In their prayers they asked for many different blessings: for the birth of a child, deliverance from their enemies, healing in sickness, the removal of reproach from God's city, for the coming of Messiah, the welfare of the ecclesias, the opportunity to preach, and so on.

Things to Pray for

So what do we pray for today? Our lives may be very different from those in Bible times, yet our true needs are the same as those of Godly men and women long ago. We could list some of them as follows:

- *Material blessings:* a source of income (however modest) that will provide food, warmth, shelter, clothing— remembering the plea of the wise man: "Give me neither poverty or riches" (Proverbs 30:8).

- *Help in Overcoming Sin:* we may have a besetting sin, a weakness that we find difficult to conquer, something that is marring our service to God. We regularly succumb and need God's help to win the battle.

- *Health:* the vigour and energy to look after ourselves and our loved ones, and assist in the work of the ecclesia; if possible, not to be a burden on others.

- ***Intercessory prayers*** on behalf of our children, family, members of the ecclesia and the Brotherhood worldwide, someone in danger or difficulty, those in the world who suffer—that their cares may be eased and that we may find opportunity to support them.

- ***The Work of Preaching:*** that those who seek may find the Gospel, and that our witness, and mission work throughout the world, may be effective.

- ***Israel and the Jews:*** that God would remember His ancient covenant, and that they might come to recognise the Lord Jesus Christ and repent.

- ***The Coming of Christ:*** that the times may be hastened, and God's purpose fulfilled; that our Lord may come with justice and judgement and set up his kingdom.

- ***Courage and Wisdom:*** that from our diligent reading of the Scriptures, angelic watchfulness, and the fellowship of our brothers and sisters, we may remain strong and faithful in whatever circumstances lie ahead.

Pray—and leave the answer to God. The important thing is that we pray:

"Is any among you afflicted? Let him pray. Is any merry? Let him sing psalms. Is any sick among you? Let him call for the elders of the church; and let them pray over him ... and the prayer of faith shall save the sick, and the Lord shall raise him up; and if he have committed sins, they shall be forgiven him. Confess your faults one to another, and pray one for another, that ye may be healed. The effectual fervent prayer of a righteous man availeth much." (James 5:13-16)

"Prove me now herewith ..."

So is there no limit at all to the list of blessings that we may ask of our Heavenly Father? God's provisions are indeed boundless:

"Prove me now herewith, saith the LORD of hosts, if I will not open you the windows of heaven, and pour you out a blessing, that there shall not be room enough to receive it." (Malachi 3:10)

"He is able to do exceeding abundantly above all that we ask or think." (Ephesians 3:20)

The Lord Jesus spoke about the gifts that his Father gives to those who ask:

"What man is there of you, whom, if his son ask bread, will he give him a stone? Or if he ask a fish, will he give him a serpent? If ye then, being evil, know how to give good gifts unto your children, how much more shall your Father which is in heaven give good things to them that ask him?" (Matthew 7:9-11)

The obvious and immediate lesson is that our Father does what is best for His children, but is there not another suggestion hidden in these words? Some of the things we ask for are, in fact, as lacking in nourishment as stones and as harmful as serpents. God, as a loving Father, will withhold such things, even though we think we want them, and will provide instead what will do us good.

Sadly, in ignorance or foolishness, many of us do pray for things we would be better without. The 'blessing' we have asked for may actually do us harm or divert us from the way of life. What then does God do? As we have just suggested, He may simply not grant a request that will do us no good: He has after all promised that He "will not suffer you to be tempted above that ye are able", and spare us from that temptation. He may, however, decide that it would be good for us to learn from our unwise choices: He may grant the request, yet lovingly ensure that we are not tried beyond our capacity—"but will with the temptation also make a way to escape, that ye may be able to bear it" (1 Corinthians 10:13).

A Pitfall in Prayer

Are there requests which we should not make? There are certainly petitions which, often with good intentions, we put forward in the wrong way. Let us illustrate this by quoting from a prayer once heard in a religious broadcast: '... humble our arrogance, calm our anxiety, give us the gift of faith.' At first, the requests sound innocent enough, but there is something wrong in at least two of them. It is true that humility is a characteristic learned from God—but God does not plant it in us; it is for us, not Him, to 'humble our arrogance'. Again, from the reading of His word, and the fellowship of brethren and sisters, our anxieties will be calmed—we do not presume that God will do it by direct intervention. And finally, though God does indeed inspire faith within us, chiefly through the scriptures, it does not come to us as some mystic 'gift'.

The Work of Prayer takes Time

We should be careful that we do not slip—however unintentionally—into such language. Requests in prayers along the lines of 'Show us thy Truth' or 'Grant us to know and love Jesus better', are not entirely unknown among us. Brethren who use such expressions almost certainly have the right intentions in mind: that from the word of Truth, by fellowship, by a lifetime of commitment as disciples of Christ, allowing God to work in us, we shall deepen our knowledge and love of the Truth—"It is God which worketh in you both to will and to do of his good pleasure" (Philippians 2:13). But that transformation will take time and it would be better to avoid language in our prayers which seems to imply that it can happen in an instant.

We shall conclude with the sound advice of Paul:

"In every thing by prayer and supplication with thanksgiving let your requests be made known unto God. And the peace of God, which passeth all understanding, shall keep your hearts and minds through Christ Jesus."

(Philippians 4:6,7)

18

THE FAMILY AND ECCLESIA

Brethren, in particular, have a serious responsibility to guide their families and lead the ecclesia in prayer. They must be ready to pray in the ordinary circumstances of life, as well as in difficult situations—when all we can do is to pray.

PRAYER starts with ourselves—our personal prayers to the Father. But none of us lives a completely solitary life: as children we are anxious about our parents and our friends and include them in our prayers. As we mature we become concerned for others, and especially (for those who marry) the one who is to become our life's companion. Those who are in Christ, moreover, are concerned about the welfare of their brothers and sisters, their ecclesias, and the work of the Brotherhood.

Marriage and Family Life

We should not need reminding of the central place that prayer must occupy in marriage and family life. In his book *Steps to True Marriage*, Brother Harry Tennant has expounded more fully than is possible here the vital importance of prayer and commitment to God in courtship and marriage, in bringing up children, and in facing all the joys, duties and difficulties of family life.

In a household blessed with marriage "in the Lord", the wife is "in subjection" (1 Peter 3:1), submitting herself unto her own husband "as unto the Lord" (Ephesians 5:22): the believing husband will therefore pray. He will consider it his duty and privilege in Christ to "manage his own household well, with all dignity keeping his children submissive, for if someone does not know how to manage his own household, how will he care for God's church?" (1 Timothy 3:4,5,12, ESV).

Husbands and Wives

Prayer and Bible reading are the vital foundations of the Godly marriage. It may sound trite but it is true: 'The family that prays together stays together'. How often, when a marriage has foundered, does the ecclesia discover—too late—that the couple have never properly learned to pray together; that thanks at mealtimes were perfunctory— that, in fact, apart from thanks for food, the husband rarely or never took the opportunity to lead the household in prayer? There will of course be times when husband and wife choose to say their own prayers, but there will most definitely be occasions when they need to pray together. It may be helpful if the two of them first discuss what they want to pray for, and if the husband then prays aloud.

In a sensitive verse about the relationship between husbands and wives, Peter makes a direct connection between prayer and marital harmony:

"Likewise, husbands, live with your wives in an understanding way, showing honour to the woman as the weaker vessel, since they are heirs with you (*or*, since you are joint heirs) of the grace of life; *so that your prayers may not be hindered*." (1 Peter 3:7,ESV; also 4:7)

Peter clearly takes it for granted that they are a praying family, and he is concerned that any lack of mutual understanding, any tension or disharmony, will hinder the performance and mar the effectiveness of prayer.

Paul also, writing to the Corinthians, mentions prayer in the context of intimate relations:

"Do not deprive one another, except perhaps by agreement for a limited time, *that you may devote yourselves to prayer*; but then come together again, so that Satan may not tempt you because of your lack of self-control."

(1 Corinthians 7:5,ESV)

A Sister's Role

There are occasions when no brother is present—where sisters live together, where a mother is on her own with the children, when sisters meet together at an ecclesial Sisters' Class, or when they take charge of Sunday School or CYC. In these circumstances, a sister will give thanks for food and offer other prayers, for in the absence of brethren she does not "usurp authority over the man" (1 Timothy 2:12).

In the presence of a brother, however, sisters follow Paul's teaching based on the principle that "the head of every man is Christ; and the head of the woman is the man; and the head of Christ is God" (1 Corinthians 11:3): in other words sisters defer to the brother to pray.

Prayer in the Ecclesia

Prayer is a responsible task. In choosing presidents for ecclesial meetings, we take particular account of their ability to lead a congregation in prayer (as well as their competence in other 'platform skills'). Of course, the president will not offer all the prayers, but he must be able, through his knowledge of the ecclesia and an awareness of the differing capacities of its members, to call on those who have the ability to pray.

Both in the ecclesia and in the home, brethren have a demanding responsibility and it may well be asked whether all are able to rise to this calling. In fact, by having such high expectations, are we in danger of intimidating those who are called upon?

That would be most unfortunate: let us never portray prayer as such an onerous task that we put off some who, perhaps through modesty rather than incompetence, do not feel sufficiently equipped. The duty of leading your brothers and sisters, friends and young people in prayer is not irksome: it should be a joy rather than a burden; it is a demanding task but at the same time a tremendous privilege—and skill comes with practice.

Public prayer is a skill to be learned: even if we have long experience it is still a task that requires careful thought in advance (and preferably prior warning from the president). For the novice it may need longer preparation—with written notes if necessary. Occasionally, in ecclesial life, some seem to be irritated by the efforts of brethren whose work for their Lord is still developing. Yet there has to be time and opportunity—and tolerance—if those capacities are to develop. Would it not be tragic if only those who are born with immense confidence and a great facility with words were to lead us, while younger, sensitive, diffident brethren were never used?

Fluency is not everything; sometimes a brother who is struggling to find the right words reflects far better the feelings of those on whose behalf he is praying—who also struggle in their approach to the Father. It is even possible that the brother who gives the perfect, eloquent prayer (if there is such a thing) may actually do his brothers and sisters a disservice, for he can make them feel inadequate. They (and he) may be so preoccupied with his clever use of language and ready quotation of Scripture that the necessary qualities of humility and insufficiency are lost. We too can be like the Pharisee in the Lord's parable, who "prayed thus with himself" (Luke 18:11).

Challenging Situations

As in all service to our Heavenly Father, there must be a harnessing of different talents, the participation of young and old, of those still developing their skills and those who are mature. We can all tolerate the odd hesitation or omission in a prayer, accepting that practice will lead in the end to the maturing of brethren who are able to meet the needs of any situation.

A beloved sister has been diagnosed with a terminal illness; a long awaited baby is stillborn; a young man has suffered an accident: few brethren look forward to presiding at the Breaking of Bread meeting on the Sunday which follows such a sad event. Even doing a reading may be difficult; the exhortation is taxing; but for the one giving the opening or closing prayer there is a special challenge. In those circumstances, it is the mature brother, one toughened and mellowed by the experiences of life—not necessarily the particularly fluent—who rises to the occasion and expresses on behalf of the stricken family and ecclesia, in simple and sincere words, what needs to be said. Similar thoughts apply to those who take a funeral service.

Tensions in the Meeting

Challenging in a rather different sort of way are those unhappy occasions when there is tension in an ecclesia, or at home; when there have been hurt feelings, and harsh words. How does one pray? How can one pray? Sometimes it may seem as if we should not even bring such things into the holy presence of God—yet that can never be right. However unworthy or mean our disputes may be, however foolish the injured pride of the parties, there is nothing that cannot be brought to God in prayer. In certain circumstances, when discussions, interviews and letters seeking reconciliation have (it seems) all failed, *prayer may be the only way forward*—though, of course, prayer must be the first not the last resort.

A family or an ecclesia in such a circumstance must prepare themselves for prayer: prayer will help and heal if it is embarked upon in sincerity and humility, in a genuine desire to let God's will prevail. We must not, as one of the injured parties ourselves, come in self-righteousness and indignation before the Almighty, asking Him to 'put our brother right'. And again, it requires a brother of the proper maturity and in the right frame of mind to seek enlightenment and forgiveness for all concerned.

God will unfailingly guide and bless those who humbly seek His help. And in the very process of bringing our problems to God in prayer we shall see them in a new perspective. Was the problem a petty ecclesial decision? By lifting ourselves on to the plane of prayer, we shall be more ready to grasp the obvious solution!

Returning to the family scene, what about a domestic crisis, an argument between husband and wife? It is impossible for the husband to pray—even to give thanks at the next mealtime—without acknowledging to himself that *he*

111

is responsible for the spiritual order of his household (see once again 1 Timothy 3:4,5,12), and admitting before his Lord that he and his wife may both have fallen short in their disagreement. By taking the path of prayer we come to see life's difficulties in a new light, even before we receive God's answer.

Praying for the Concerns of the Brotherhood

So much can be achieved if brothers and sisters join together in prayer. A brother in Eastern Europe was called up for military service and the outlook was bleak: he could have been compelled to serve or face hard labour. Ecclesias worldwide heard of the situation and prayed earnestly that a way out of the situation might be found. In the case we have in mind, relief came when a medical condition made the brother ineligible for military duty.

We should similarly pray for the easing of troubles in the Brotherhood. There may be concern over the actions of a brother or an ecclesia; the decisions of a committee; or the views expressed in a magazine article. Such feelings are natural, and to a degree healthy, for we should certainly test and discern what is going on in our community; and sometimes, inevitably, we shall not agree with what others say and do. But what action do we take?

It is unhelpful simply to complain about the affairs of the Brotherhood in our own family or ecclesial circle—or, worse, to form a faction promoting an opposite opinion. The better way is to reflect on what Scripture (and the *Ecclesial Guide*) teaches on the subject; to approach the individual or organisation directly in the spirit of Matthew 18:15-20; and to pray. How often have we deplored what a brother or an ecclesia or a committee has done, but have not thought to bring the matters to God in prayer? If someone else is wrong, they need help; if we are wrong, then we need help!

19

THE PRAYERS OF THOSE OUTSIDE THE COVENANT

Those in covenant relationship have privileged access to God, but the stranger too has always been able to approach Him. Children may also learn to pray, for God has commanded His people to come with their families before Him.

ISRAEL were called to be a holy people, separate from the nations, and in a special relationship with the LORD their God: "If ye will obey my voice indeed, and keep my covenant, then ye shall be a peculiar treasure unto me above all people ... a kingdom of priests, and an holy nation" (Exodus 19:5,6). In Abraham they had been brought into covenant relationship with God; while the priesthood, feasts and sacrifices of the Law of Moses gave them privileged access to His presence.

Covenant Relationship

So what of the stranger who was not in covenant relationship with the God of Israel and who was not under the Law? If Israel were God's chosen people, then it might be expected that other nations, not chosen by God, would be excluded from worship and prayer. If God could say through Amos, "You only have I known of all the families of the earth" (3:2), then it would seem that other peoples, outside the covenant, had no claim on the God of Israel.

There were, however, arrangements whereby the stranger could be brought within the fold of Israel. In connection with the passover, for instance, God said:

"There shall no stranger eat thereof ... When a stranger shall sojourn with thee, and will keep the passover to the LORD, let all his males be circumcised, and then let him come near and keep it; and he shall be as one that is born in the land."

(Exodus 12:43-48; cf. Leviticus 22:10-13)

Throughout the Old Testament there are examples of foreigners finding sanctuary within the congregation of Israel; and in the New Testament we encounter many proselytes who, joining in temple or synagogue worship, would have engaged in prayer.

But what of strangers who had not taken such steps? Clearly they could not participate in feasts and formal worship, but were they excluded from access to God in private prayer? Some have quoted an incident in the life of Abraham as proving that this is so. Through a misunderstanding, Abimelech had taken Sarah, but God intervened and instructed him:

"Restore the man his wife; for he is a prophet, and he shall pray for thee ... So Abraham prayed unto God: and God healed Abimelech ..." (Genesis 20:7,17)

Integrity of Heart

It is true that this "stranger" was outside the covenant and it was right that Abraham should pray on his behalf; yet in fact Abimelech had already prayed to God, as verses 3-7 show. First God (or an angel) spoke to him; then Abimelech responded, pleading that he had acted in integrity and innocency; and finally God answered him, acknowledging that he had acted "in the integrity of his heart" (verse 5). This passage, far from demonstrating that one outside the covenant cannot speak with God, actually proves the opposite.

On the other hand, Job prayed (at God's command) on behalf of his friends, whose hearts were evidently not right before God:

"The LORD said to Eliphaz the Temanite, My wrath is kindled against thee, and against thy two friends ... Go to my servant Job, and offer up for yourselves a burnt offering; and my servant Job shall pray for you: for him will I accept ... And the LORD turned the captivity of Job, when he prayed for his friends." (Job 42:7-10)

Even in this example, we note that God addressed Eliphaz, so that communication between the Almighty and those who displease Him is not excluded—as we see when God speaks to heathen kings.

"Concerning a stranger ..."

But to reinforce the truth that God hears the prayer of the stranger who approaches in the right frame of mind, we only have to look at Solomon's prayer at the dedication of the temple:

"Concerning a stranger, that is not of thy people Israel, but cometh out of a far country for thy name's sake ... when he shall come and pray toward this house; hear thou in heaven thy dwelling place, and do according to all that the stranger calleth to thee for: that all people of the earth may know thy name, to fear thee, as do thy people Israel." (1 Kings 8:41-43)

Turning to the New Testament and to the experience and teaching of the apostles, there is a new situation—though the principles are unchanged. The question of prayer no longer relates to whether men and women are ritually within the Law of Moses, but whether they are in Christ.

Proselytes and God-fearers

The Acts of the Apostles records the conversion of many Gentiles. Some, like the Ethiopian eunuch, knew the Hebrew scriptures and (though we are not told specifically) doubtless prayed to Israel's God: he needed only minimal instruction to acknowledge the work of Christ and his mediatorship in prayer.

The example of the centurion Cornelius is interesting. He was not a full Jewish proselyte (who were circumcised and obliged to keep the whole Law), but a 'God-fearer', who believed in the one God of the Jews:

"... a devout man who feared God with all his house-hold, gave alms generously to the people, and prayed continually to God ... he saw clearly in a vision an angel of God come in and say to him, 'Cornelius'. And he stared at him in terror and said, 'What is it, Lord?' And he said to him, 'Your prayers and your alms have ascended as a memorial before God ...'"　　　　　(Acts 10:2-4, ESV)

Quite clearly, then, an uncircumcised Gentile (cf. Acts 11:3) could pray to God; the prayers of Cornelius were heard; he was baptized—and on the strength of his conversion the apostles in Jerusalem concluded, "Then to the Gentiles also God has granted repentance that leads to life" (11:18, ESV).

"Aliens from the commonwealth of Israel"

But what about Gentiles who were neither proselytes nor God-fearers? There were many indeed who had no previous contact with Judaism and yet learned of Christ. As Paul writes to the Ephesians:

"At that time ye were without Christ, being aliens from the commonwealth of Israel, and strangers from the covenants of promise, having no hope, and without God in the world: but now in Christ Jesus ye who some-times were far off are made nigh by the blood of Christ ... through him we both have access by one Spirit unto the Father. Now therefore ye are no more strangers and foreigners, but fellowcitizens with the saints, and of the household of God."　　　　　(Ephesians 2:12-19)

Though they had been "without God in the world", they had learned of the Gospel. And how had they learned? As a result of the preaching, certainly; but also in many cases surely because they had been praying, if only to "the unknown God", seeking for truth. Paul, in fact, encourages us to understand that God made all men with a natural inclination, too often suppressed in a godless world, to seek after Him. To the men of Athens he said:

"God ... giveth to all life, and breath, and all things ... that they should seek the Lord, if haply they might feel after him, and find him, though he be not far from every one of us." (Acts 17:24-27; see also 15:17)

Then, as now, there were men and women who were looking for more than the idolatry and materialism of the age offered and, perhaps not knowing what they sought, or of whom they sought it, prayed fervently and sincerely for enlightenment. It surely still happens today, and by angelic guidance or whatever means, God answers the unformed and ill-informed prayer and guides the searcher to the Truth. Facing shipwreck, Brother John Thomas—at that time still "in an uncertain state of mind"—resolved, "as the waves were closing over him, to go down with the prayer on his lips, 'Lord, have mercy upon me for Christ's sake'" (*Dr. Thomas: His Life and Work*, page 8).

Praying at a Public Meeting

Let us move on from considering those individuals outside God's covenant who seek Him in prayer, to the situation of the believer who prays on their behalf. What is the position of the brother who is called upon to pray in a meeting where there are interested friends at different stages in their search for truth? Some may have a knowledge of the Gospel and sufficient understanding to say a meaningful "Amen" to the prayer; others may still be in ignorance of the basic elements of the Gospel. That was the position Paul found himself in, just before the shipwreck on the journey to Rome, when he apparently saw no problem in leading his fellow-mariners, but "gave thanks to God in presence of them all" (Acts 27:35).

The brother who prays—for example, at a meeting in an ecclesial hall, or at the launch of a campaign—will modify his prayer according to his audience. What both Old and New Testament examples have shown is that, while all may "seek after God" in prayer, there is a distinction between those who are in covenant relationship with God and those who are not. When we pray on behalf of an assembly which includes some who have not yet truly learned of God as a Father, we cannot properly address God as "Father" as we would when all those present have been brought into this new and intimate relationship. It is also difficult in a mixed company to use a phrase such as "in Christ's name", because strictly this applies only to those who are "in Christ"—those who have "named the name of Christ" (2 Timothy 2:19). On the other hand, it is only through the Lord Jesus Christ that anyone has access to God, so that it is right to acknowledge in some suitable way that a prayer, even on behalf of those who are still 'seekers', ascends to the throne of God by virtue of Christ's work: the phrase "for the sake of Jesus Christ" may be the one most appropriate for this purpose.

The choice of hymns should also concern presidents: not all hymns are appropriate for those not yet in Christ. In times past, brethren may have been over-zealous in regard to the matter of worship in the presence of 'the alien', but we could profitably be more conscious today about the way we pray and sing with those not yet within the household.

Children and Prayer

This brings us to the subject of children's prayers—first of all, prayers offered on behalf of children, and then prayers formulated by children themselves.

We are guided by a number of specific scriptures, but also—and most importantly—by the general principle that God deals with families, including the little ones. The LORD God revealed Himself to Abraham and Sarah, but took for granted that they would also instruct their children:

> "For I know him, that he will command his children and his household after him, and they shall keep the way of the LORD." (Genesis 18:19)

Israel, similarly, were to teach their children:

> "Ye shall teach (these words) to your children, speaking of them when thou sittest in thine house, and when thou walkest by the way …" (Deuteronomy 11:19)

When Israel appeared before the LORD their God, it is clear that they came with their families:

"Gather the people together, men, and women, and children, and thy stranger that is within thy gates, that they may hear ... and that their children, which have not known any thing, may hear, and learn to fear the LORD your God."   (31:12,13)

These passages lay down the basic principle that children learn of God by being present when their parents read, pray and worship: they see and hear what mother and father (and uncles and aunts) do in their service to God. They hear the prayers offered on their behalf, prayers which seek blessings on the family; prayers which ask God (as the years of maturity approach) to bless them in their enlightenment so that in due time they are ready to acknowledge Christ.

With children, observation leads to imitation: a very young child, even with limited understanding of spiritual truths, can believe in God and can give a simple prayer— usually a prayer of thanks for parents, friends, possessions, experiences etc.; a prayer containing innocent requests; occasionally even a prayer prompted by illness or distress.

Ishmael, Samuel, Josiah

Does God hear such prayers? Did He not hear the cry of Ishmael? The angel said to Hagar: "God hath heard the voice of the lad where he is" (Genesis 21:17; see also Exodus 22:22,23). God spoke to "the child Samuel" (more likely a youth, but still growing in the faith), and Samuel responded in humble awareness of God and with a willing heart. Three times he heard a voice and ran to Eli, and only on the third occasion did Eli realise that it was the LORD speaking—and he told the child what to say:

"And the LORD came, and stood, and called as at other times, Samuel, Samuel. Then Samuel answered, Speak; for thy servant heareth."   (1 Samuel 3:10)

And doubtless the young Josiah, made king at the age of eight, feared God and prayed to Him: "For in the eighth year of his reign, while he was yet young, he began to seek after the God of David his father" (2 Chronicles 34:3).

The Teaching of Jesus

Jesus commended the simplicity of children as an example for his disciples to follow: "Suffer the little children to come unto me, and forbid them not: for of such is the kingdom of God" (Mark 10:14). He clearly believed that children could praise God: "Out of the mouth of babes and sucklings thou hast perfected praise" (Matthew 21:16; Psalm 8:2). And more significantly still, Jesus suggests that children can have a relationship with God through the angels: "Take heed that ye despise not one of these little ones; for I say unto you, That in heaven their angels do always behold the face of my Father ..." (Matthew 18:10).

The example of Jesus himself (even allowing for the fact that he was an exceptional child) must tell us something about the way a child's mind can be attuned to God. In the temple at the age of twelve, he was "about his Father's business" and as he grew to adulthood he "increased in wisdom and stature, and in favour with God and man" (Luke 2:49,52).

God hears prayer. We have noted previously that His ears are closed to those whose sin and wilfulness exclude them from His presence; but He hears all who seek Him with a contrite heart, and desires that they will find the true path of prayer, and eventually come to Him through Christ.

20

HOW AND WHEN TO PRAY

We need to pray regularly, undisturbed, briefly or for a longer time. Believers have kneeled, stood, bowed the head, or lifted up their eyes. We approach, not with eloquence or emotion, but with dignity and reverence before our God.

PRAYER is a serious undertaking. Those who pray are venturing into the presence of the Holy One, and this cannot be done casually. Though we may pray in any situation—not only at the meeting but at home, at work, at the wheel of a car, in a moment of panic or a time of pleasure—we should still understand that we do not lightly address Almighty God. There are many aspects of prayer which prompt genuine questions for the disciple:

Where is the best place?

For the Lord Jesus it was sometimes a mountain top (Luke 6:12), though more often probably the corner of a room. For Peter it was "upon the housetop" (Acts 10:9). Lydia prayed "by a river side" (16:13). Some have the ability to come into God's presence in the busiest of places but most people pray more effectively away from distraction. Kneeling at the bedside is a good option—better, surely, than trying to pray in bed where we may fall asleep.

What is the right posture?

The Bible shows us faithful believers standing, sitting, kneeling, bowing the head, lifting their hands etc. Joshua, pleading for Israel, "rent his clothes, and fell to the earth upon his face before the ark of the LORD until the eventide"

(Joshua 7:6; cf. Numbers 16:22; Ezekiel 9:8; 11:13; Revelation 11:16). Hannah stood to pray (1 Samuel 1:26). Elijah "went up to the top of Carmel; and he cast himself down upon the earth, and put his face between his knees" (1 Kings 18:42; cf. Ezra 10:1). David lifted up his hands (Psalm 28:2; 141:2; cf. Lamentations 2:19). Solomon stood before the altar (he also kneeled) and "spread forth his hands toward heaven" (1 Kings 8:22,54; cf. Ezra 9:5). Paul exhorted "that the men pray in every place, lifting up holy hands …" (1 Timothy 2:8, RV).

Others "bow the knee" (Isaiah 45:23; cf. Ephesians 3:14) or "bow (down) the head" (Genesis 24:26; Exodus 4:31; 1 Chronicles 29:20). Different Hebrew words suggest differing degrees of obeisance, according to whether the worshipper 'bowed the head', 'stooped', or 'went on bended knee'. Daniel "kneeled upon his knees three times a day, and prayed, and gave thanks" (6:10); while Jesus, Stephen, Peter and Paul are all recorded as kneeling in prayer (Luke 22:41; Acts 7:60; 9:40; 20:36; 21:5).

Whereas many formerly kneeled in churches, most of us feel it is right to stand in prayer, with heads bowed — though others raise their heads and even their hands, following Old Testament precedent. Should our eyes be closed or open? Children — and adults — are less likely to be distracted if they close their eyes. On the other hand, perhaps the psalmist's eyes were open when he lifted up his eyes to the hills (Psalm 121:1; cf. 123:1). And perhaps the Lord's eyes were sometimes open when he prayed to his Father (John 11:41; 17:1).

When should we pray?

The Jews had particular times for prayer. "Evening, and morning, and at noon, will I pray", said David (Psalm 55:17). Peter prayed "about the sixth hour" (Acts 10:9); Cornelius was praying "at the ninth hour" (10:30; cf. 3:1). (These times were counted from 6 a.m. not 6 p.m.) Jesus "continued all night in prayer to God" (Luke 6:12).

In our day, there can be no fixed times for prayer — but regularity is important. However pressed for time we may be, we should not start the day without prayer. We surely desire to seek our Father's presence at some time, or times, during the day; we pray at mealtimes, and we set aside time for devotion and prayer in the evening—with a final prayer before we sleep.

But—if we worry that such a schedule is impracticable—we are not bound by a timetable: prayer is the more fulfilling if it is spontaneous. There will be an unscheduled moment in our day when, between mundane tasks, we can shut out the world and turn to God, offering thanks and seeking His blessing.

In Silence or Aloud?

There are many hints in Scripture that individuals raised their voice and cried aloud to God in prayer: "I cried unto God with my voice ... and he gave ear unto me" (Psalm 77:1). When we are with others we pray aloud but on our own most of us pray silently. There is something to be said, however, for praying aloud even when we are alone: it helps to prevent our minds wandering, and we may make more effort to order our thoughts and be more precise with our words if we have to voice them. We shall, moreover, hear ourselves speaking to God and that will help us to realise how small we are, and how insignificant our requests must be to the infinite God.

For how long should we pray?

Moses "fell down before the LORD ... forty days and forty nights" (Deuteronomy 9:18). The congregation of Israel must have stood for several hours while Solomon prayed at the dedication of the temple (1 Kings 8). We think of the example of Anna, who "departed not from the temple, but served God with fastings and prayers night and day" (Luke 2:37); the example of the apostles who resolved to give themselves "continually to prayer" (Acts 6:4); and also Paul who laboured "night and day" in prayer on behalf of the believers (1 Thessalonians 3:10; 2 Timothy 1:3). And there is, of course, the vivid lesson concerning persistent prayer in the parable of the importuning friend (Luke 11:5-13).

God's watchmen are commended to "keep not silence, and give him no rest" (Isaiah 62:6,7). On the other hand, Jesus warned against "vain repetitions" and "much speaking" (Matthew 6:7), and condemned those who "for a pretence make long prayers" (Mark 12:40). "Let thy words be few", said the Preacher (Ecclesiastes 5:2). God will always listen to the humble child of God—like the tax collector—but not to those who are just talking to themselves—like the Pharisee (Luke 18:10-14).

"Pray without ceasing"

"Pray without ceasing" (1 Thessalonians 5:17); "Men ought always to pray" (Luke 18:1); "continuing instant in prayer" (Romans 12:12); "praying always with all prayer and supplication" (Ephesians 6:18; cf. Colossians 4:2). Scripture teaching is clear, yet most of us recognise that we do not "pray without ceasing". We acknowledge with admiration those few who make it their mission to be beacons of prayer on behalf of the Brotherhood. At some time, whether once a week, or once a year, they will mention in their prayers the names of every one in their ecclesia; and in addition dozens, perhaps hundreds of other fellow pilgrims, the aged and the children, and interested friends. They will have a care for the world, and pray that suffering may be alleviated, and the days shortened. Their untiring work is rarely acknowledged and we may not even be aware of it. As for the rest of us, we perhaps would not welcome too close an audit of the time we spend in prayer.

How frequently we pray, and for how long, will depend very much on our temperament and our circumstances. The point about 'unceasing' prayer is not that we are always on our knees, but that we have minds regularly, if possible constantly, attuned to spiritual things and conscious of God's presence.

Should one fast before intense prayer?

Fasting, sometimes in sackcloth and ashes, was a sign of penitence and often preceded prayer (Judges 20:26; Ezra 8:23; Esther 4:16; Jonah 3:5,6). Before Barnabas and Paul set out on the first missionary journey, the ecclesia at Antioch "fasted and prayed, and laid their hands on them" (Acts 13:2,3). But Jesus warned that fasting was not for the purpose of impressing your fellow-men: "Anoint thine head, and wash thy face; that thou appear not unto men to fast, but unto thy Father which is in secret" (Matthew 6:16-18).

We may be far removed from the culture of sackcloth and ashes; we do not rend our garments. Yet we should certainly not dismiss the idea of fasting. It is an act of self-denial and discipline; fasting changes our perspective and our priorities and helps to clear the mind. But it should not be insisted upon, because for some it may itself become a distraction, and undermine rather than aid concentration.

One of the benefits of fasting is that it calms the spirit, removing from our restless minds the tensions and preoccupations of our lives. But this calming of the restless mind must be our aim even if we do not fast. Prayer can never be fully effective if we are rushed and tense, preoccupied by a dozen other things waiting to be done. Prayer is not a job on a list of jobs, to be ticked off before we move to the next! Nor are we ready for prayer if there is bitterness in our soul: we have to put away grudges, and forgive all hurts *before* we approach God. This may be what Paul means when he refers to the "lifting up of holy hands, *without wrath and disputing*" (1 Timothy 2:8, RV).

A Generation Gap?

The basic principles of prayer never change, but some aspects of the way people pray may differ from culture to culture, and from generation to generation. We have noted that in past ages there were those who approached God "in sackcloth and ashes". We observe today how ultra-orthodox Jews chant their prayers with movements of the body and bowing of the head. And we acknowledge that there are differences of style and approach even between generations of Christadelphians: an older generation prays in more formal language, using phraseology based on the Authorised Version of the Bible, while some of a new generation adopt more everyday language.

There are those of us who are attached to the traditional style; others who feel that God is to be addressed, not casually, but in the forms of speech that our children and our neighbours will understand. Whether, for example, to use "Thee" and "Thou", or "You" and "Your", for God is a matter that has, at times, led to sharp differences of opinion in ecclesial life. Here, we shall not make a firm proposition either way: the use of traditional rather than contemporary phraseology is a question of personal choice rather than a doctrinal issue. An older generation may need to learn tolerance of today's less formal prayers; equally, a younger generation should learn to appreciate why others prefer a more formal style: yet each must seek to show respect and humility.

Eloquence and Emotion

Prayers offered at our meetings sometimes seem half-hearted, downbeat, lacking passion and joy. Should we not try to pray with greater emotion? Do not the psalms and prayers of great men and women of God suggest that there is a place for eloquent and sometimes emotional language?

Most would agree that a little more fervour in our communal prayers would be a good thing: it would stir us up if brethren prayed with greater intensity. On the other hand, there is a danger of being carried away with emotion. A brother giving a prayer may well be on the verge of tears, but it does not help the congregation if he breaks down.

Maturity

God does not seek cleverness with words but, rather, the thoughtful petition of the mature believer. Instinctively, we can recognise the prayer of a mature brother: he is often, though not necessarily, older in years; he will speak from deep wells of spiritual experience; he will pray with intimacy yet profound humility. His language may show passion, but he will never be flamboyant; his voice may tremble in the true fear of God, yet his words will be expressed with the confidence of the full-grown disciple. He has learned to pray a little after the pattern of his Lord.

21

PROBLEMS IN PRAYER

We may lack faith; we may feel we are not the 'praying sort'; we cannot find the time; we feel unworthy; we have sorrow in our lives which gets in the way of prayer. But with help, we shall learn to meditate, pray, and trust in God.

THE first obstacle to prayer is doubt: we need to have faith that prayer works. A young child has total confidence in the ability of Mum and Dad to do anything and everything. That is the child-like trust we need to develop in our relationship with our Father—the inward conviction that He really will hear us. When the disciples failed to cure an epileptic boy, Jesus explained that it was "because of your unbelief: for verily I say unto you, If ye have faith as a grain of mustard seed, ye shall say unto this mountain, Remove hence to yonder place ... and nothing shall be impossible unto you" (Matthew 17:20).

Doubt ... and Faith

The sad implication for all of us is that we barely have the faith equivalent to a grain of mustard seed. If only we had faith, all things would be possible. In Mark's account of the above incident, we hear a little more of the conversation that took place between Jesus and the father of the epileptic boy:

> "All things (said Jesus) are possible to him that believeth. And straightway the father of the child cried out, and said with tears, Lord, I believe; help thou mine unbelief." (Mark 9:23,24)

Seeing his son healed, the man would from then on have had much greater faith. So it is with us: through our experiences—and the experiences of others—we gradually increase our faith. We may commence with doubts, but let not those doubts stop us praying: once we have begun to see that God answers our prayers, our doubts will start to disappear and our confidence will grow.

'I am not the praying sort'

Some disciples are naturally inclined to pray; others find it very hard—and feel guilty. It does not help us in our life of prayer constantly to feel guilty. The desire to pray varies considerably from one disciple to another: some, without any shame or blame, are not the contemplative sort. They are committed, sincere believers, but they are more at ease joining in communal prayers than praying on their own.

We have to face the fact that we are all different. Some pray a lot, and others only a little. But can we leave it there? Surely, with encouragement, example and the good advice of others, those who may not at first feel able to pray can learn. It may come slowly but with God's blessing we shall grow in our capacity and desire to speak to Him through Christ. We learn to relax, to clear our minds of the 'noise' of busy lives, to concentrate on the things of the Spirit; to cultivate the focused mind that we see in David, and especially in the Lord Jesus Christ.

'I cannot find the time'

Many complain that they cannot find the time for prayer. The pressure of life today is largely to blame. Though our forebears worked long hours, they learned amid the daily chores to set aside times for prayer and devotion. In the commotion and cacophony of today's world we are in danger of losing the facility, and even the desire, to commune quietly with our God, and reflect on the wonder of our relationship with Him through Christ.

We owe it to our Father, to our families, our ecclesias and ourselves, to do something about this situation. Management courses, designed to train executives in the wise and effective use of their time, stress the need to be able to withdraw from the 'shop floor' and reflect undistractedly on the larger issues of running the enterprise. This is a good analogy for disciples, who desperately need to find opportunity, not just for attendance at meetings, but for prayer (on their own and with the family), meditation and personal study. (It goes without saying that we are not distinguishing here between brothers and sisters, for both have this urgent need.)

'I cannot concentrate'

Brethren and sisters sometimes worry about what they see as their inadequacies in prayer. For example:

- I want to praise and thank God but my words sound trite and insincere;

- I start to pray, but cannot concentrate; I find my thoughts wandering;

- I can pray for two minutes, but feel that my prayer is quite inadequate; yet if I go on for ten minutes I must be wearying both myself and God.

There are no 'instant' solutions to these problems. Yet the Scriptures do give us guidance in the discipline of prayer. The fundamental problem is that we feel we have to formulate, all at once, a complete and spontaneous prayer—and yet we cannot find the words. For many, the answer is to be found with the help of meditation. In fact, the pattern of meditation and prayer that we saw in Psalm 19 (see page 41) is an example of what we could attempt ourselves—not trying to imitate David exactly, but adapting his method to our own situation.

Why not, then, write down on a piece of paper a list of, say, five things in our surroundings to marvel at: it might be the hills and streams in our locality, the birds on the bird table, or simply the flowers in a vase: even the city-dwellers among us must see aspects of the natural world that give glory to God. Let us focus our thoughts on these—opening our eyes to look at them, if that helps—*and praise God for them.*

Follow this, as David did, by contemplating God's more abstract blessings (which, again, we could write down): the riches of His divine revelation to us, the knowledge of the Gospel of salvation, the wonder that we have been called. This is almost bound to make us feel inadequate before God, and we shall start to think of our shortcomings and sins—and our need for forgiveness. So what began as meditation soon turns into supplication—*prayer*! We have discovered the discipline of reflecting on God's works, and then addressing Him in prayer. Other petitions then follow, again interspersed with meditation.

"In the time of trouble"

We may have trouble in our lives; there may be people with whom we have difficulties. Turn, then, to Psalm 27 and use that psalm as a pattern for our own attempts at disciplined prayer. Notice, again, how David moves in and out of meditation mode:

- He starts by meditating upon his God, the strength of his life: "The LORD is my light and my salvation; whom shall I fear?" (verse 1);

- He talks about his adversaries: "When the wicked, even mine enemies, came upon me ..." (verses 2,3);

- But then he turns to think about the "one thing" that he desires, "that I may dwell in the house of the LORD ... to behold the beauty of the LORD" (verse 4);

- He declares his confidence in God: "In the time of trouble he shall hide me ... mine head shall be lifted up above mine enemies round about" (verses 5,6);

- And, having meditated in this way, he *prays:* "Hear, O LORD, when I cry with my voice" (verse 7);

- Then come those familiar words, "Teach me thy way, O LORD" (verse 11);

- Finally, having commenced with meditation, having continued in prayer, he now concludes in meditation: "Wait on the LORD: be of good courage, and he shall strengthen thine heart" (verse 14).

Our sentiments will not be those of David but, again, we can adapt this model to our own circumstances: we can *marvel* at the glory of God; *meditate* on the blessings and guidance He has shown in our own life and the lives of those around us; *acknowledge* the difficulties we are experiencing; *recognise* our inability, on our own, to solve our problems; *trust* that God can do all things; then, in prayer, *commit* our ways to Him, and *ask* for His help.

Meditation thus prepares us for prayer; it helps us to banish bitter thoughts; it assists us to discipline our minds; it enables us to focus our thoughts without worrying about our ability to pray, or feeling guilty that we may be wearying God. Meditation should help us to crystallise what we want to ask our Father. Having meditated, we then proceed to ask—and He will hear. In the way that is best for us, He will respond to our petitions.

'I cannot pray'

Yet it may be that some disciples find it difficult to meditate and, in certain circumstances, impossible to pray. They may feel unworthy, hurt, confused. Friends or family (if they know the situation) should offer counsel and comfort, emphasising that even if the person has lost faith in mankind, or even in themselves, they need never lose faith in God. If prayer, for the moment, is difficult, then why not just read a psalm, or a hymn?

There are psalms and hymns for all circumstances, and the rhythm of familiar scriptural words should start to soothe the spirit and restore the necessary confidence to resume prayer.

If thou but suffer God to guide thee,
    And hope in Him through all thy ways,
He'll give thee strength whate'er betide thee,
    And bear thee through the evil days;
Who trust in God's unchanging love
Build on the Rock that naught can move.

What can these anxious cares avail thee,
    These never-ceasing moans and sighs?
What can it help, if thou bewail thee
    O'er each dark moment as it flies?
Our cross and trials do but press
The heavier for our bitterness.

Only be still, and wait His leisure
    In cheerful hope, with heart content
To take whate'er thy Father's pleasure
    And all-discerning love hath sent;
No doubt our inmost wants are known
To Him who seeks us for His own.

Sing, pray, and keep His ways unswerving,
    So do thine own part faithfully,
And trust His word; though undeserving,
    Thou yet shalt find it true for thee:
God never yet forsook in need
The man that trusted Him indeed.

                                    HYMN 147

22

DOES GOD ANSWER?

Nothing is too hard for the LORD. God heeds, He hears, He answers prayer. The answer will be according to His will and we have to accept that, even when our wish seems so right, what God decrees may not always be what we desire.

ARLY on in this study (chapter 5), we drew up lists of Bible synonyms for prayer, and discovered a rich variety of words—both in English, and in the original Bible languages—to do with our approach to God. With such a rich vocabulary for *man's approach to God* in prayer, it is hardly surprising to find that the vocabulary to do with *God's response* to prayer is similarly varied.

God "answers", "hearkens", "heeds", "regards", "remembers"—in fact, we can draw up another table of Bible words (see next page) used (in the AV/KJV) in connection with our Heavenly Father's acknowledgement of His children's prayers. In the psalms particularly, a wide range of expressions are used when pleading for God's answer:

> "*Give ear to my prayer*, O God; and *hide not thyself* from my supplication. *Attend unto me*, and *hear me*."
>
> (Psalm 55:1,2)

> "*Keep not thou silence*, O God: *hold not thy peace*, and *be not still*, O God." (Psalm 83:1)

In earlier chapters we have met an impressive number of men and women whose prayers were answered—patriarchs, priests, judges, prophets, kings, mothers in Israel, apostles of Christ. Hannah received the child she prayed

---

TABLE 3

BIBLE WORDS FOR GOD'S RESPONSE TO PRAYER

Answer	Hide not Thyself
Attend	Hold not Thy peace
Be entreated	Incline (Thine ear)
Be not silent	Keep not silence
Bow down (Thine ear)	Listen
Forget not	Look down
Give ear	Make haste (to help)
Have respect	Regard
Hear	Remember
Hearken	Show mercy
Heed	Turn unto (me)

---

for; Nehemiah was remembered; Simeon saw God's salvation; the ecclesia in Jerusalem were guided in choosing Matthias. All of these would agree with what James wrote: "Tremendous power is made available through a good man's (or woman's) earnest prayer" (5:16, J. B. Phillips).

Dramatic Interventions

James follows that statement with an example from the life of Elijah. Before a faithless Israel, he desired God to show Himself mighty and confound the prophets of Baal: "Let it be known this day that thou art God in Israel, and that I am thy servant, and that I have done all these things at thy word." When the fire of the LORD "consumed the burnt sacrifice, and the wood, and the stones, and the dust, and licked up the water that was in the trench", the people acknowledged, "The LORD, he is the God; the LORD, he is the God", and Elijah was vindicated (1 Kings 18:36-39).

The answer that Elijah received was far more immediate and dramatic than he had dared to imagine: even as he asked for God's help, "the fire of the LORD fell". And it consumed not just the animal, but the wood, the stones, the dust, and the water in the trench. God so often gives an answer "above all that we ask or think".

God may be at work before we pray. There is the story of a person in great distress because of a debt that had to be paid by a certain day, and he decided it was time to pray for financial help: that help came by the next post—in the form of a cheque that had been posted *before* the person prayed! Many of us, however, when asked to give an example of answered prayer in our lives, tend to hesitate. The reason is that we are trying to think of some special occasion when a prayer to God was *dramatically* answered. The fact is that answers to prayer are not always dramatic: God works in mysterious ways in the smallest aspects of our lives—and we should be quick to acknowledge this. If someone asks us if God has responded to our prayers, we should unhesitatingly tell them that God's good hand has been upon us hourly, daily, at every stage of life, keeping us from harm, guiding our decisions. Surely we believe that God was in control?

How God works is beyond our comprehension: He speaks to us in His Word; His angels encamp around us; He provides companions to strengthen us; He even brings trials to test us. By very ordinary happenings our ways are directed—if we have committed them to our Father. It could be an unexpected telephone call, a change in the weather, a casual meeting: the smallest thing can prove to have been a turning point in our lives. God may *occasionally* give us 'signs' that, for example, the job we are hoping for is the right one; but we cannot demand it. Pray rather that circumstances may work out according to the divine will:

> "We know that *all things work together for good* to them that love God, to them who are the called according to his purpose." (Romans 8:28)

'Unanswered' Prayer

Some prayers are *not* answered. The reason (in retrospect, at least) may be evident: "Ye ask, and receive not, because ye ask amiss" (James 4:3). Often we shall have cause to thank our Father that the 'blessing' we asked for was not granted, for now we realise that it would not have been good for us.

Jesus in Gethsemane prayed: "Father, if thou be willing, remove this cup from me …" What if God had granted that request? Our salvation would not have been achieved! Thankfully, we know that the Saviour himself drew back, for he added, "nevertheless not my will, but thine, be done" (Luke 22:42). God understands when we ask for the wrong thing, and gently guides us in the better way.

But sometimes it seems as if very worthy and unselfish prayers are not heard. We can accept a negative answer to requests that were for our own benefit or comfort, but some petitions were for another's good—and we trusted we had asked "according to his will" (see 1 John 5:14). How could a prayer for an interested friend, a possible new lightstand, the healing of a brother essential to the continuance of an ecclesia—how could these not be according to God's will?

Jesus must have prayed constantly for a stiff-necked people: not all of those prayers were granted. Paul doubtless prayed fervently for a particular convert, or for the establishment of a certain lightstand, and was refused. When we are refused, the only thing we can say is that it is not God's will—at this time. The answer to prayer, as many have learned humbly to accept, may be Yes, No, or Wait! "Is anything too hard for the LORD?" (Genesis 18:14). No; but the answer we desire may not be in His eternal plan.

"How inscrutable are his ways!"

One path of consolation in the face of unanswered prayer is to consider this: if all was perfect in this life, if all our desires were met, and every prayer was answered, our need and longing for the kingdom might be that little bit diminished. The more we have now, the less urgently we desire the blessings of that future age. There is no easy way to explain the 'unanswered' prayer. Often we are left wondering, not fully comprehending the ways of God: "How unsearchable are his judgements, and how inscrutable his ways!" (Romans 11:33, ESV).

23

"AMEN"

"Amen" is our assent to a prayer: we say it to associate ourselves with all that has been said, agreeing that it reflects what is true, steadfast, sure and faithful. Jesus was called "the Amen", for he was "the faithful and true witness".

THE prayers we bring before the throne of grace vary enormously in their style and content, but they generally have one thing in common: they conclude with the word "Amen". There may be no Scriptural command that we *have* to say "Amen" at the end of a prayer, but there are good precedents. After bringing up the ark, David offered a psalm of thanksgiving, "And all the people said, Amen, and praised the LORD" (1 Chronicles 16:36). Paul, concerned about the hazards of speaking in tongues, asks: "How can anyone … say 'Amen' to your thanksgiving when he does not know what you are saying?" (1 Corinthians 14:16, ESV).

"So be it"

In both Old and New Testament times, the children of God expressed assent to a prayer by saying "Amen", a Hebrew word which has passed, untranslated, into English and many other languages. And the use of "Amen" was not limited to prayers. When the Levites stood on Mount Ebal to utter the curses, the people said "Amen" to each in turn:

> "Cursed be he that removeth his neighbour's landmark. And all the people shall say, Amen."
>
> (Deuteronomy 27:17 etc.)

137

Nehemiah had to call an assembly of the returned exiles to examine certain grievances, and when he "took an oath of them"—

"All the congregation said, Amen, and praised the LORD." (Nehemiah 5:13)

They were simply saying, 'So be it'. There is in fact one place (in Jeremiah 11, in the AV), where the Hebrew *Amen* is translated "So be it". Interestingly, the passage picks up the language of Deuteronomy 27, as God says: "Speak unto the men of Judah … and say thou unto them, Thus saith the LORD God of Israel; Cursed be the man that obeyeth not the words of this covenant …" And just as Israel had said "Amen" to all the curses at Mount Ebal, so now Jeremiah responds:

"So be it (*amen*), O LORD." (Jeremiah 11:2-5)

Some modern translations, such as the NIV, in fact render the phrase, "Amen, LORD."

The God of Truth

But there is more to the Hebrew *amen* than mere assent. There is an occasion in Isaiah 65 where *amen* is rendered "truth":

"He who blesseth himself in the earth shall bless himself in the God of truth (*amen*); and he that sweareth in the earth shall swear by the God of truth (*amen*)." (Isaiah 65:16)

And the meaning extends beyond 'truth'. Amen is one of a family of Hebrew words—*emeth, emunah, aman, amen*—used in the Old Testament to convey 'steadfastness', 'faithfulness' and 'truth'; something that is 'right', 'established', 'sure'.

These, then, are the vibrant overtones of the simple word "Amen". In saying "Amen" to a prayer, we are associating ourselves with what we believe to be true, faithful and steadfast. In fact, the passage in Isaiah 65 would encourage us to go one step further and suggest that when we say "Amen" we are associating ourselves with the God of Truth;

we are committing our prayer, in faith, to the God of stead-fastness and faithfulness. Amen is a short word, yet with deep spiritual meaning.

"The faithful and true witness"

The New Testament carries over the Hebrew idea of Amen, and indeed the word itself. Where the Lord Jesus Christ so often introduces his teaching with "Verily", he will have used the word *amen**—assuring us that his word, too, is faithful, steadfast and true:

> "For all the promises of God in him are yea, and in him Amen, unto the glory of God by us."
>
> (2 Corinthians 1:20)

Our Lord inherits the names and characteristics of his Father, so that the angel could say to John, in the letter to Laodicea:

> "These things saith the Amen, the faithful and true witness, the beginning of the creation of God."
>
> (Revelation 3:14; see also 19:11)

All that was faithful and true in the Father is revealed in the Son—and in those who show forth a measure of that same faithfulness and truth in their own lives.

An Audible "Amen"

Strictly, of course, in view of what we have said, it should be the congregation rather than the one who prays who say the "Amen". In practice it is normal for the one praying to say "Amen", thus signalling the end of his petition—and so long as this is done modestly, it is acceptable. It is not for the one who has prayed to give a loud "Amen": that is for those who have listened to, and now give their assent to the prayer. Actually, it would be good if we were a little less inhibited about this; if our "Amens" were rather more audi-

---

*It is interesting that where Matthew 16:28 and Mark 9:1 have "verily" (*amen*), in the same context Luke 9:27 has "of a truth" (*aletheia*), demonstrating once again that *amen* carries the meaning of 'truth'.

ble in our meetings. There is, of course, a balance to be struck between an "Amen" which is scarcely audible and an "Amen" in which each member seems intent on outdoing the other in vocal intensity and which may miss the point.

The Future—God will dwell with Man

Prayer is God's wonderful provision for this time of probation. In the fulness of time, prayer as we know it now will no longer be required—in the age when "the tabernacle of God is with men, and he will dwell with them, and they shall be his people, and God himself shall be with them, and be their God" (Revelation 21:3).

But communication with God does not then cease: those blessed with immortality will worship God and the Lamb; they will rejoice and sing eternally in a life of divine fellowship and praise. This is the future to which we aspire:

"After this I looked, and behold, a great multitude ... from every nation, from all tribes and peoples and languages, standing before the throne and before the Lamb ... crying out with a loud voice, 'Salvation belongs to our God who sits on the throne, and to the Lamb!' And all the angels were standing round the throne and round the elders and the four living creatures, and they fell on their faces before the throne and worshipped God, saying, 'Amen! Blessing and glory and wisdom and thanksgiving and honour and power and might be to our God for ever and ever! Amen.'"

(Revelation 7:9-12, ESV)

24

EPILOGUE

SO we come to the conclusion of these studies. Much more could be said, for this is an infinite subject. Some may feel we have only started to scratch the surface, but it is hoped that what has been written may help especially the new disciple to set out on the path of prayer, and those of longer experience to be encouraged along that path.

The Conclusion of the Matter

What features of our subject stand out? Surely we must acknowledge first of all *God's great desire* that His children come to Him in prayer. That in turn must be reflected in *our desire* to pray: prayer should be a privilege, and never a chore. Faced by the challenges of today's perplexing world, and the difficulties we experience in our ecclesias and at home, prayer is the best—and often the only—path open to us.

Though we feel inadequate to the task of speaking to the Almighty Maker of the universe, we shall in fact learn by persistence in prayer that He hears and answers the humblest disciple. We need no special gift; our Father demands no impressive eloquence; He hears every cry and knows the longings of each heart, even if they are unexpressed—or inexpressible.

We may pray on our own but we do not pray in isolation: even in the seclusion of our home, in the silent preoccupations of our own mind, in trouble or in joy, we are always in the company of ten thousands of the saints who wonder and meditate, who worship and sing, who present their petitions and plead God's mercies. When King Darius signed his decree, and the enemies of Daniel found him—undeterred—praying in his chamber, is it not significant that, although he was alone, "his windows were *open toward Jerusalem*" (Daniel 6:10). We must not be introverted in our prayers: we gain strength from knowing that we are part of a greater number, present and past, who have had the windows of their minds always open toward Jerusalem, their thoughts and prayers constantly attuned to God's purpose.

Fed from the Word

And that brings us to a vital truth: that a life of prayer is a life founded on and fed from the Word. The reading of the Scriptures will keep us in touch with the great principles of prayer, and with Biblical examples of men and women of prayer. The psalms, the prayers of the Lord himself, the prayers we find in the epistles—all these, and others, will instruct us in the habit and power of prayer.

"Give to the winds thy fears;
Hope, and be undismayed;
God hears thy sighs and counts thy tears:
God shall lift up thy head ...

Through waves, and clouds, and storms,
He gently clears thy way;
Wait thou His time, so shall the night
Soon end in joyous day."

HYMN 346, VERSES 1 & 5

SCRIPTURE INDEX

SUBJECT INDEX